keys to our heart

a prelude
to the
sixth root race

by Nick Scott-Ram

keys to our heart

Copyright © 2002 by Nick Scott-Ram

Published by
LIGHTWORK·MEDIA
P.O. Box 600
Candler, North Carolina 28715 U.S.A.
1-800-335-1382

Designed by
Paula Chance
1170 N. Highland Ave., A-10
Atlanta, Georgia 30306 U.S.A.

Library of Congress Control Number: 2002107023
Scott-Ram, Nick. 2002
ISBN 1-887343-83-0

Printed in the United State of America.
First Printing 2002
10   9   8   7   6   5   4   3   2   1

Dedication

To David Cousins
A Divine Teacher
With love, light and thanks for the bananas.

Contents

Synopsis

The cosmic, planetary, and life-form changes that are now occurring are all part of a new energy vibration, or frequency wave, that is surging through the Planet. Increasing numbers of people are being affected by these new energies, and are waking to the call of the Divine within themselves. These new frequencies are moving all of us — from our minds to our hearts — and this transformation marks the beginning of the Sixth Root Race.

The Root Races represent the basic blueprints for experience and expression over given time periods here on Earth. Each Root Race is characterised by a series of different aspects or qualities. As the Fifth Root Race draws to a close, the emergence of the Sixth Root Race is being heralded by major changes in how we connect with our hearts. Connecting with our hearts means opening new doorways within ourselves, connecting to the Divine within each of us, and connecting with the huge array of new frequencies and energies around us, both on the physical and other dimensional planes.

Keys to Our Heart explores some of these new connections, including the Paramatman Light (or Divine Light) and the Avataric Network, the matrix of new crystalline energies, how to open new doorways within our heart, and the emergence of our true divinity. *Keys* also explores how we can build bridges between our heart and the huge array of different life-forms that co-exist with us, not only on the Planet, but also on levels of awareness different from our own. Accessing a deeper comprehension of what is within each of us, how our heart connects us to the Divine, and how this divinity is present in everything, *Keys to Our Heart* shows the way to unlocking these new frequencies, and how to unite our heart with the diversity of life around us — thereby accessing "unity through diversity".

The substance of the book has been channelled through guides, and in particular through guidance arising from what may be termed Dragon Energies. The Dragon Energies combine the twin frequencies of Love and Power, and as the Planet, and all life on it, wakes up to the new call of Sixth Root Race living, so it is that the Dragon Energies within it are being re-awakened.

Keys to Our Heart deals with the awakening and transformation that many people feel they are going through, and, in particular, emphasises the deepening connection to the Divine within all of us. It also explains why these changes are happening, and perhaps, above all, it shows people how best to align themselves with the changes for spiritual growth. *Keys to Our Heart* also shows how things might be in the golden age that we have all been promised.

Acknowledgements

The nature of this book makes it impossible for me to acknowledge each and every individual who has contributed to the informational matrix of energy of which this work is an outcome. So to all those whose names are not mentioned below — you know who you are. Please accept my love and my thanks.

The greatest debt I owe is to David Cousins, who, from my first meeting with him, and during the subsequent years that I have been fortunate enough to have attended his workshops, has shown me an entirely different perception of the physical world and inner planes. His love, wisdom, compassion and understanding have taught me many things. David truly woke me up and without him this book would not have been possible.

My second debt of gratitude is to Frances Travis, who has shown me great love, patience and understanding in my endeavours. I am extremely fortunate to have found a partner who is keen to explore the different realms of reality, and whose spiritual understanding is a rock of inspiration.

I would like to thank Cornelia Selkirk, for being a great friend who has shared much of my spiritual journey in recent years. Cornelia helped provide feedback on early drafts, and I would also like to thank her for allowing me to use the beautiful painting for the front cover of this book.

I owe a very big 'thank you' to Trish Miller, who undertook the arduous task of editing the manuscript and putting it into a more digestible form. This was no simple matter, and I have very much appreciated Trish's expertise, commitment and dedication. Her role has been invaluable.

A special 'thank you' to Ann Leigh, and to her guide, Gallecto. Ann's guidance and understanding of the workings of the inner planes, as well as her openness in connecting with Gallecto, have been of great benefit to me. Ann's encouragement and assistance in editing early sections of the book were also very helpful.

A number of other people, including Vaune Newcomb Hodgetts and Claude Randall, read early drafts of the manuscript and gave invaluable feedback.

I would like to thank a number of people with whom I have been fortunate enough to work in recent years. It has been a real pleasure and privilege to share energies and experiences with them, and to work in a more collective way. They include Liz Barratt, Candice Bishop, Maria Bowden, Jess Chen, Juan Angel Diaz, Alan Gauld, Jean Hettiaratchi, Derek and Wendy Jenkins, Emma Jenkins, Matt Jenkins, Lotta Kelliher, Bernadette Kissane, Dona Lipscomb, Yolanda Lopez, Douglas and Joanne McGlashan, Teresa Meagher, Tracy O'Sullivan, Avril Remon, Ernesto Piscini, Traudl Platzer, Sabine Schlichting, Peter Selkirk and Elizabeth Walton. My apologies if I have left anyone out.

Finally, I would like to say a huge 'thank you' to Baluthra and his friends, for the opportunity of channelling their special energies. It has been a wonderful experience to feel the diversity of frequencies and informational patterns flowing through me, and to trust the process of starting off with a blank piece of paper, not having a clue as to what will come through! I would also like to thank the numerous guides who have worked on the inner planes to bring through the energies into me and who have assisted me along all stages of my path.

Author's Introduction

This is a book about the heart and the ways in which our hearts can open, expand and connect with the new energies that are now gracing the Planet. I feel somewhat fraudulent in calling this an 'author's introduction', since in truth, I did not really write *Keys to Our Heart*. This book has been channelled through a series of guides, although the main instigator is a Dragon Guide called Baluthra. At best, I have acted as a channel for the energies to come through me. The energies and what is communicated by these energies in the written word, have all come from what I would term the 'inner planes'. These planes are substantially larger than the physical planes, and represent different dimensions of awareness and consciousness, and are the home of many different energies. Attempting to grasp, let alone understand what these planes are, is often beyond the capabilities of our intellectual mind. These planes of different dimensional awareness, energy vibration and consciousness can only be accessed through experience. We have to train our awareness to remember some of these energies, and use our body, in all senses of its perception, as a tuning-fork. In this way, my awareness and physical vehicle have been used as a tuning-fork to resonate with, and bring through these Dragon energies from the inner planes.

The Dragon energy is an energy that is external to the human personality. In this context, when I talk of the Dragon energy, I am also referring to it as a 'guide'. Guides come in many shapes and forms (and are not limited to the human form) and are generally beneficial to us. Some people are more familiar with Native American guides. Guides can also be experts in different activities, such as healing or channelling or trance states. Many people are not aware of these inner guides because they have not developed a strong enough connection with them. However with practice, it is relatively easy to build up a stronger connection with your guide. I certainly found it something of a surprise to connect more deeply with some of my guides, and to find that a 'felt sense' of their energy was in fact very familiar to me. They had been with me all along, and I hadn't realised it.

My first contact with a Dragon guide was several years ago. During one particularly deep and powerful meditation, I remember feeling a large winged presence. There was a great sense of love and calm that also came through in this meditation. I was also fortunate enough to have been prepared for this experience through working with a friend and colleague, Ann Leigh, and her guide Gallecto. Their love and under-standing played a critical role in enabling me to find an anchor point.

In connecting with my Dragon guide, I began to explore what the Dragon energies meant for me. Some of my subsequent meditations were accompanied by the flapping of wings and encirclement of my sub-tler bodies by my guide's wings. What I also came to understand was that a part of me is 'Dragon-like'. This was shown to me in a very poignant way in one meditation. As part of this meditation I visualise putting on a 'dragon robe' which tunes me into the Dragon energy. This robe is a structural thought form generated by imagining a dragon being wrapped around my physical form, rather like an overcoat. Some way into the meditation, I saw in front of me a large crystalline building. I approached the building and went inside. Once inside, I saw my dragon body. It was dark green, had wings and I also knew that it could change colour. My dragon body felt very ancient. During this experience I also experienced the whole of my body tingling with energy. As I went deep-er into the meditation, I found myself going back to an old Planet which was inhabited by dragons. I knew immediately that this was an old 'home' planet. The planet was dark and there were many dragons flying around. I ended up merging with one of them and experiencing much more directly the distinctive dragon energies. The whole sequence was like opening up an ancient doorway within myself — what could be called a 'dragon doorway'.

Following on from this experience, I learnt to allow my dragon guide's vibration into my heart centre, and to begin to merge and meld more deeply with him. The Dragon energy is of a very particular vibration and at its most pure, stands for the twin pillars of love and power. In connecting with my guide, I could always sense these energies. It was interesting that my guide gave me his name fairly early on in our exchanges, although it wasn't until sometime later that I came to trust what had come through. Baluthra, as my guide calls himself, has a very particular vibration which I could always recognise. And so, as is often the way, one thing led to another and after several months I was starting to channel Baluthra. I certainly was not expecting to write a book, although Baluthra did indicate that we would have a lot of work to do. So it was, that in effect I sat down one day and just started channelling Baluthra. This book is the finished product of that process.

My role in this enterprise has been to remain as clear as possible so that I can access those energies that are passing through me, and at the same time express these energies through the written word. While the words may act as a hook to interest you, the main business of this book is contained in the energy pulse *behind* the words. This may sound strange, but in connecting with these energies, I hope that you may experience some of the deep joy and love which I have found in this connection. The energy expressed in *Keys to Our Heart* works directly on the heart and as I have read and reread sections of the writings, I have found my heart centre at times expanding, and the energy working on other centres in my body. This is connected with the capacity that we all have to varying degrees — which is to be as open as possible to the Divine within us, and to act as a channel for these energies.

What do I mean by Divine energies? Well, the Divine or God means different things to different people. It is said that there are as many paths to God as there are grains of sand on a beach. Each of us has a unique path to God or the Divine. It is this path or journey which is so special and which should be respected. What is being offered in *Keys to Our Heart* is the opportunity to connect with a different level of

awareness of what is in our own heart. In connecting with this awareness, in an open and clear way, there is the possibility to connect with
what lies beneath the veil for each of us. This connection is not an intellectual one and I would urge against reading the book in a purely aca-
demic way. Rather, to get the most out of it, I think it is best to read it
intuitively — to feel parts of it that resonate with you, to explore these
parts and to allow the connections to be made, however unusual these
connections may seem at first.

Making these connections and allowing them to form requires
trust — trust in yourself and trust that maybe you are not deceiving
yourself or letting your so-called imagination run away with you. In the
end, the quality of the *feeling* will talk to you about the authenticity of
the connection that you have made — it will feel right or balanced. So,
in connecting intuitively, or with your *heart*, I hope that you may get a
sense of the underlying energy in *Keys to Our Heart*.

The way the energy works in the book, on one level, is rather like
the ocean tides or swells. The tides rise and fall, and so it is, in my experience, that the energies ebb and flow, pulsate, move rapidly and then
more slowly, and then more rapidly again. These energies are not linear,
but rather feel more like an ever-moving helix. In the early parts of the
book, topics are touched on as an introduction, and then are returned
to in more detail later. In this way the energy builds.

This is not to say that the *words* are irrelevant or need not be
considered. Not at all. It is that the words are rather like the surfer
on the crest of a wave. The wave is the underlying energy, the surf board
is the apparatus of the mind which helps to 'translate' the energy into
thoughts, and the surfer is given the joyous task of tracking, bobbing
and weaving, and following the waves of intent as they form, disappear
and reform again. In short, the surfer is the written word. By its very
nature, channelling can never be one-hundred percent accurate. At its
simplest, channelling is opening oneself up — to one's inner voice, to
one's intuition, or to different levels of connection and expression. The
clearer one is in one's mind, or the emptier one is, the more accurate

the flow of energy and information.

Although we may not recognise it, there is a very real sense in which we all channel. In opening ourselves up to what is around us — whether it be in our dreams, our aspirations, our ideas, our intentions, our feelings of connection with different people, or our connection with Nature — there is a real sense in which we are just being a channel. Ultimately, we are channels for Divine energy — the trick is to recognise it and to get our mind out of the way. No easy task. It is for this reason alone, that no channelling is ever fully accurate. This is also another reason for suggesting that it is more beneficial to connect with the underlying energy than just the words. However, it should not be forgotten that the words will have their own vibrations and may well help to unlock or act as keys to opening aspects of ourselves up.

Before finishing, I want to point out a few features of the way the book has been set out. First, there are sections of the book which are indented and marked with a vertical rule line. In the editing process, it has been especially difficult to find a balance between the different styles of channelling which have come through. There have been a number of different guides contributing to the book, each with their own way of presenting things. In order to separate out some of these different styles, principally between the Dragon guides and other sections which have been channelled, the selective indentation of passages has been used. The passages which have been indented represent the more direct channelling from the Dragon guides.

Another tricky area has been the need for a consistent policy for capitalisation of words. I have attempted to follow the conventional policy of reserving such usage for proper names, the Deity and His immediate attributes. In a number of places where the subject matter is directly addressing the Divine or God, this has proved more difficult due to the potential for a plethora of capitalisations. I have attempted to find a balance and hope that it is acceptable to the reader.

I am also acutely aware in reading sections of this book, that the terminology may appear unfamiliar or opaque. I have therefore included a glossary at the back of the book to give additional information on some of the more frequently-used terms and definitions. In addition, I have added notes to each of the chapters where I have tried to clarify or exemplify what is meant by some of the passages, phrases or words. It is often difficult to give fixed or comprehensive definitions to some of the more elusive concepts, and the reader may also have his or her own view on the definitions. I leave the final judgement to your intuition.

Finally, it just remains for me to thank you, the reader, for taking the time and trouble to read this book. I very much hope that you find something of interest in it. If the energies touch you in some way, then the efforts of all concerned will have been a success.

Nick Scott-Ram
August 2001

Chapter 1 • Introduction

There are numberless universes and countless planes. Each universe and each plane can be subdivided hundreds of thousands of times, so that for example, within each plane there is a sub-plane, and within each sub-plane a further set of sub-planes, and so on. As we advance through the different planes, the steps taken are usually incremental and over many lifetimes. Experience is the key to spiritual evolution: each soul, through incarnation in matter, seeks as diverse an array of experiences as possible. There are lives spent in abject poverty, lives spent in resplendent wealth, and yet more with modest means and wealth. Given that this is but one axis of experience, if you multiply it by the number of different nationalities, different countries, different races within each country, it is clear that there are many diverse frequencies to be sampled. And then, of course, there is the question of coming into physical form as either a man or a woman. How many times have we given birth to a baby? Millions of times. So on one level we come into incarnation afresh, although in reality our body remembers previous experiences from earlier incarnations. This is what gives us the individual and truly specific karmic charge which is unique to each one of us, and which is a major formative factor in the evolution of personality.

While modern science tries to explain everything in terms of statistics and generalisations, which in turn can be used to elucidate so-called laws, the reality for each individual incarnating on the Planet is very, very different. Statistics are meaningless. Why do I experience one illness as opposed to another? Why do I become ill? Why should such an experience happen to one person and not another? In truth, it is the exquisite specificness of karmic interactions which makes the 'play' on the Planet so interesting. The trick, the real purpose, is to untie these karmic knots and release oneself from restrictions.

How can this be done? Well, it is not easy. It requires perfect timing, perfect conjunctions of places, people and planetary energies. This may appear daunting, but usually things have a way of turning out 'for the best' when one's own intuition is in play. Many people know about synchronicity, the conjunctions of events and 'accidents'. This is just scratching the surface: the conjunctions and synchronicities in one's life should flow naturally when one is in tune with one's heart, and the object of the exercise is to use all circumstances and connections to unbind karmic charges, and to be at the right place, at the right time, to fulfil one's karmic destiny.

It is as if we were blind-folded, except that in a way *all* our senses are dulled or dampened. The use of our body memory can help us to see through the blind-fold, and a deeper perception of how our own body energy[1] reacts lends impetus to this 'x-ray vision'. The process operates on many different levels, and we shall seek to explore some of these.

Connecting with our Heart — Through Compassion

In order to free ourselves from pre-determinism and a loss of spontaneity, we have, in one sense, to lose our mind, i.e. to lose the shackles that bind us to logic. It is this movement, this shift from the mind to the heart, that is the key to the whole process.

What do I mean by 'connecting with our heart'? This is at once both extremely simple and difficult. The simplicity lies in being open to our *self* — to being honest with our self, and our feelings and intuitions. The body, in one respect, is like a giant tape-recorder. Every experience, every feeling, is recorded in our body fluids, our organs, our tissues, our bones, our cells and our DNA. It is possible to access this information, although the process requires patience, caution, care, and above all, compassion. It is this bringing of the heart into oneself, in a true and deeply compassionate way, that can help to unlock some of the memories held within the body.

Why is compassion so necessary? Because it is really the only tool that can help us bridge the gulf of separation. I refer not only to the initial separation between the mind and body, which some may recognise as the Cartesian split or dualistic stance[2], but also to the separation between our body and our feelings. For many, experiences are not properly integrated within their system. We experience, but do not always digest. Then we file away the product of the experience, often in an incomplete form. Some people say that they are sure they have processed something, and that it is therefore no longer an issue. Since there are so many levels of human experience, this is rather similar to saying that an understanding of basic arithmetic will automatically enable one to understand quantum mechanics. The depth and multiplicity of layers of experience mean that what may seem resolved on one level, may not be cleared at another. The situation is reminiscent of an iceberg, where what lies below the surface of the water is much greater than what is above. This is not meant as a criticism — it is merely the beginning of a realistic perception of the complexity of life as we live it. Rather than experiencing an absolute clearance, what we normally receive is that which we can handle at any given point.

After a period of time has elapsed, we can view a similar problem from a slightly different angle. This suggests that we have shifted; sometimes substantially, often imperceptibly. Then, when an opportunity to connect with the original blockage or problem presents itself, we are in a position to see it from another perspective, and to react differently.

Another way of looking at this is to compare the situation to a helix. We may start at the bottom of the helix, and slowly circle around a problem, removing some of the charge associated with it. We then spiral up to a slightly higher level, where we can view the problem from a different perspective, gain a broader understanding, and see that it has a different set of features. In this spiralling, and with increased cognisance, we can connect with, and process, the issue at a deeper level. It is thus both an 'upwards' spiral and a 'downwards' motion, as we see the problem more clearly. The two processes go hand-in-hand, and are a reflection of a universal process or law.

The key to the release of a problem (which can also be experienced as trapped energy) is compassion. Bringing one's heart energy to what is locked in the body or mind, or both, is fundamental to a proper alignment of oneself with the issue. This compassionate alignment is the catalyst for profound releases at many levels: just as the mind can separate, the heart will unify and bring together.

The Soul's Journey — A Forever-Changing Path

The journey of the soul through time and space is a complex one. Nothing is linear, and what may appear as circumstantial is often planned, down to the minutest details. Take, for example, the case of a farmer. He may cultivate his land for years and years. One year, the seeds that he has normally planted fail to grow because of a drought or some other climatic changes. The farmer worries, and wonders what to do, then he tries other seeds, and there is growth again — a shift has occurred. Nothing is static.

Change can be painful. It can also be uplifting and strengthening, and the journey of the soul through all of its incarnations is predicated upon change, and yet more change. That is the one constant, apart from birth and death. Change is a continuum — it has no beginning and no end. It simply is. It is all a question of perspective. For most people, the perspective is that we are solidly rooted in third-dimensional reality, and that this mundane world is our ultimate existence. Yet nothing could be further from the truth. If we shift our perspective to regard the passage of our soul as passing through millions upon millions of lives, then the importance of what we do in the 'here and now' takes on a different meaning. We do not only have one life. We are eternal. We have journeyed over many aeons in space and time, and the human form is but a local one. We have been through so many others: the dragon, the bird, the alligator, the reptile, the elephantine form, and so many more. Each of these frequencies and vibrations is locked in our form, and is accessible to us. To access these frequencies is to open up doorways to the past, present, and future. It is these dimensional doorways which are a key to our new beginnings; the rebirth of the Planet at this time.

Many different beings currently wish to connect with Earth, and making contact with them will dispel our prejudices, and show that things are never what they seem — at all. Race, colour, and creed disappear into insignificance when one is confronted by a totally different sentient life-form. It is important to remember this, and to embrace it, because it will allow a 'shattering of the veil' to take place. Many books have been written about how we have been duped on this subject; how there are cover-ups and conspiracies. That may or may not be so, but what is important is to unlock your own reality by travelling within, through your own inner doorways. This will help you to connect with yourself, and to discover who you really are. For sure, no one is just a human being; as previously stated, everyone has incarnated in a range of different life-forms. What we 'are' now is simply the local fashion. This is the ancient wisdom, the knowledge that is now being understood by many of us.

Frequency Signatures

'Frequency' plays a significant role in all of this, and in this context it has more than one layer of meaning. It is primarily the resonance of the energy-vibration emitted by each of us. This changes on a daily basis, dependent upon how our body feels: happy or sad, tired or relaxed, healthy or ill. Behind this is a secondary signal; a deeper, more resonant frequency, that is indicative of the totality of our subtle[3] or ethereal bodies. This signal is correlated with the degree of light and darkness within our overall being. The higher the frequency, the lighter we are, whilst slower-frequency people resonate at a lower vibration. In our daily activities, there is always a trade-off between the different frequencies emitted by people. Some people feel more comfortable in a specific frequency. It is a mistake to think that a particular frequency is good or bad, and to attach value judgements to these frequencies. Remember that we have all spent many lives operating at lower frequencies. It is only through this wealth of experiences that we earn the right to the higher vibrations which allow us to be flexible. We can thus cope with both the high and the low frequencies, just as a versatile singer can access either high or low notes. Each type is necessary, and both high and low frequencies are integral to God's Plan.

Given that we all emit a frequency, and each have our own 'signature', there remains much flexibility within a lifetime over how we utilise these frequencies, which can be likened to experiences. If one takes a single lifetime, for example, as representing a given frequency, and then adds all the frequencies from past lives, this constitutes an impressive array of experiences. Connecting with any one frequency within ourselves can allow access to a different part of ourselves of which we were unaware before, so these frequencies can be seen as doorways to different aspects of ourselves. With practice, we can shuttle between them, connecting with the different aspects of ourselves. It takes a little practice to do this, and more will be said about it later.

As we begin to access the different frequencies, we can build up a different picture of ourselves, a rather bigger and more interesting picture than may have been envisaged. We might sample the frequencies held within us of the Native American Indians, the Atlanteans, the Lemurians, and the Egyptians, indeed of all of the Root Races, and their various offshoots of which we have been a part. There is now a need, more than ever, to understand and access this information, as most incarnated souls comprise the Fifth Root Race. As the age of Aquarius begins, it is time for the majestic transformation into the Sixth Root Race.

The Emergence of the Sixth Root Race

Unlike previous transitions, where there has been something of a cut-off between each successive Root Race, the situation here is exquisitely different. This is one of the reasons why there is such excitement around Planet Earth at this time. The Fifth Root Race will begin evolving into the Sixth Root Race during our lifetime. This process is likely to take a number of generations. However, the changes necessary for the transformation will be significant for each generation. So every individual has to make a radical shift in his or her frequency to accommodate the new energy; the vibration and thought form that is the Sixth Root Race. This is something of a challenge. It pre-supposes our ability to connect with the older, unwanted frequencies that are in our system, flush them to the surface, release them, and replace them with new, upgraded frequencies of the Sixth Root Race 'energy package'.

Hence, many people are undergoing major, and often painful, transformations. The transformation into the Sixth Root Race is rather like travelling down a road, thinking you are going in one direction, and suddenly finding that you are moving 'in reverse' in a completely different one, without actually having a clue as to why this is so. We have thus to reverse out of the solar plexus centre into the heart centre, and this represents something of a paradox. The emotions are generally held in the solar plexus: some have termed this the 'graveyard of the emotions', because many people become trapped in their emotions, and remain unable to move through them. However, in connecting with emotions or frequencies, we can access different aspects of ourselves, because emotions, especially our deeper ones, act as gateways into ourselves. The paradox arises because we need to find a way to connect with our heart while still retaining the capacity to feel and experience emotion. In other words, life's journey often requires us to move through our emotions into our heart. This means finding a place for acceptance and alignment, rather than denial. This is the balancing trick, seen from one perspective, which is part of this transformation. I say *part* of the transformation, because it is multi-dimensional in that there are many different levels involved.

The Mind of One

In the beginning all was One: the perfect prime state, as it were. Then God decided to segregate facets of His Consciousness, turning this segregated Awareness into form, on the many different planes. Thus the process of involution[4] and evolution[5] began. As the Fifth Root Race draws to a close, all who are incarnated on the Planet are very fragmented. The multiple soul aspects of themselves, which have been built up through many incarnations, are separated, and need to be reintegrated. This fragmentation is also seen in people's everyday survivalistic patterns, and it is obvious to many, that there is an imbalance, an over-emphasis on the individual. There is such an extreme state of segregation on the Planet at this time, that the transformation into the Sixth Root Race requires a reunification, and a return to a greater sense of oneness: what can be termed the collective will as opposed to the individual will. This, on one level, is what is meant by the 'Mind of One'.

On a deeper level, the 'Mind of One' is a reflection of the Divine Will, of God's Will, to reunify the Planet and to bring about a drastic shift in the frequencies. Thus, the Mind of One is being brought into existence now, and has as its physical reference point all those souls who have incarnated on the Planet, and who are committed to working with the light and the Divine Spark. It is through the merging and unity of purpose and action of light workers (i.e. those who work with the light) that the Mind of One is being brought into existence, and why It is integral to the Sixth Root Race changes. Once formed, the energy pulse of Divine Fire that will be channelled through the Mind of One will be awesome: the conjunction of different soul families, the merging and connecting of all these beings into one force, directed and co-ordinated by God, through the Mind of One.

So the Mind of One is a reflection of God's Will, and a vessel through which His Divine Intent can be seeded into the Planet, in the physical plane. Many people are currently unaware of this; unconscious of the Mind of One, and that they are a part of all this, and have a role to play in its unfolding. Their 'sleep' is so deep that the various 'wake-up calls' made during the last few decades have failed to rouse them from their slumbers. This awakening is the remembering, the realisation of who and what they are, and of how they can be of service. To remember is to *be*, and to *be* is to serve and to irradiate. This is what needs to be understood. So the wake-up calls become more extreme, somewhat akin to standing at the bedside of a slumbering friend and shouting 'wake up!' with a megaphone at full volume. It is hardly surprising that a few people wake up with headaches!

So what of this Sixth Root Race? How will it look? What will it feel like? This channel had a dream recently, which gave him a sense of the Sixth Root Race and what it meant to him. The dream runs as follows:

I am standing on a train and it draws up at a station. I get off the train to wander around the platform. After a time the train starts to draw away and I am unable to get back on it. I am blocked from getting on it by a man, possibly a guard. As the train draws away, I wonder what I am to do.

I suddenly find myself in this vast expanse of green countryside. There is not a soul about, and no animals — just small, undulating planes of grass, stretching into the distance. I then find myself lifting off the ground. Dusk is approaching, and it is a beautiful evening sky, made up of pinks, greens, oranges, blues and violets. As I fly perhaps fifty to a hundred feet off the ground, the grass remains green, and is dotted by a few large trees. I fly up and go higher — several hundred feet higher. It is a beautiful sensation of freedom, flying above the countryside as the sun sets and the evening draws in. After a time, after many miles, I come down at a small village or town in a hilly area. It is night, and I touch down near a restaurant, a kind of pizza place, but old-fashioned in appearance. The night sky is dark blue, and the stars twinkle brightly. I go inside — the people appear friendly. Close by, one or two people seem to be arguing, but it does not matter. Somehow, behind the superficial, there seems to be a heart connection between these people.

I then find myself in a room, surrounded by a group of people. I have not met them before, but there is such a strong feeling of love between them, and a real vibration in the heart centre of everyone there. It feels like a really high vibration. Even if there were disagreements or arguments between these people it would not matter, because of the heart connection between them. I then say to them that I understand why this is so — that they are all part of the Sixth Root Race. They reply "yes", smiling at me. I feel a part of the love. A very beautiful feeling.

Accessing New Heart Vibrations

The key will be the level of vibration of the heart. This does not apply just to our own heart centres, but also to the heart centres of all living beings, as well as of the Planet itself. The planetary vibration[6] is increasing at great speed, and has moved from eight to its present level of twenty-six: and it is still climbing. This progression will continue to at least seventy over the next ten to twenty years. Since the heart centres of all living organisms are tied in with Earth's heart centre, it is clear that everyone's heart centre is going to be stretched beyond anything that can be imagined now. In practice, this means that the frequencies of the heart, the love frequencies, will be much finer. They will be encoded into our subtle[7] DNA at the light level, which is beyond the atomic level, and will be part of the major shift. There will, of course, be very substantial glandular modifications to the pituitary, pineal, third eye, ajna[8] centres, thymus and thyroid, and to other areas such as the spleen and solar plexus. All of these will effectively be 'refitted' to accept the higher-frequency vibrations.

In effect, our physical vehicles will be re-equipped to accept the new, higher vibrations. These adjustments will allow us to communicate within the waves of these vibrations, and to tune in to them. This may not appear much on the surface, but the truth of the matter will lie in our experience of it, which will not be three-dimensional, but multi-dimensional. Our awareness will expand significantly, our ability to sense, feel, and connect will be greatly enhanced, and our ability to merge and connect more telepathically with each other will be increased.

Part of the difficulty for many people will lie in their expectations of what this all means. People imagine, perhaps, that telepathy has to occur in a particular or specific way, such as 'being on the telephone' to someone else. In truth, they will experience communication differently in themselves, within a place that they are not accustomed to using. This will be a new part of themselves, although in fact it is an ancient place, which is being reactivated. These changes will be complemented by other significant differences; most importantly, the position of our existence. This awareness will be centred in the heart, rather than in the mind — as it currently is. The heart will unify, rather than segregate. It will bring together the human family under the Divine Will, and allow the next splendid level of planetary evolution to unfold. This has been foretold and will be magnificent in all of its aspects. It will be a reunification of the heart and the head. The Mind of One will become One.

Releasing Slower-Frequency Energies

Many changes are afoot. As the various dimensional doorways in the Planet open, ever wider, there will be a significantly greater influx of photon energy. This is already happening and is bringing more refined energy into the Planet and all life-forms on it. It is not simply a question of raising the vibration or frequency-level of the human species: it applies to all animals, plants and minerals. This is why different crystals are becoming activated, and why there is nowadays a much greater emphasis on vibrational medicine. The new light coming into the Planet is bringing in new energy fields, new information, new subtle technologies; and by technologies I do not mean scientific technologies, but technologies of the inner planes, technologies of awareness and expression, and above all technologies of the heart. These patterns will increase, and will be reflected in the increasing pulse rate of the planetary heart.

It is not surprising that there is such upheaval, and that many people are experiencing great extremes of emotion. Typically, they may experience the depths of depression in one moment, and the heights of ecstasy in the next. This is both interesting and significant, since these mood swings are, on one level, keys to our frequencies, since they represent a means of removing the slower ones from within us. However, having released these frequencies, there is little point in putting them back into the system. It would be analogous to an industrial company reducing its waste output from industrial processes, yet still pouring industrial waste into a river and polluting it, and then washing its hands of the responsibility because it is out of sight and out of mind. This slow-frequency energy needs to be handled differently. It requires a new way: one that is more responsible and transformational. The new way requires that the energies be offered up to the light, back ultimately to their Source, where they can be used in a more effective and (to us) informative manner.

How can we bring this about, when we have such trouble in acknowledging or recognising these slower-frequency energies in our space? In one sense it does not matter whether or not we can acknowledge them. By simply offering up slower-frequencies to the light, to God, to the highest Source of Divinity that we can connect with, irrespective of whether or not we are consciously aware of them, we shall set the process in motion. Energy follows thought, and invoking this approach will mean that on one level or another, it will begin to happen.

In truth, we all come from God, and will eventually all return to God. So everything that we do, everything that we experience, is God's in the first place. We don't own these experiences nor do we own life. It is more that they are on loan to us, and that all can be returned to the rightful Owner, at any instant of our existence. So whenever we access lower-frequency information, and slow-frequency energy deposits in our system, all we need to do is to send it into the light. We send it to our highest Divine connection, with love, asking that the energy be transformed safely, and in accordance with the highest Divine Plan. This may sound odd at first, and also counter-intuitive, but with practice it can become second nature, and will effect a profound transformation on our everyday life.

Becoming a Channel for the Divine

We can tackle our everyday problems and difficulties in a similar way. Most of us have been brought up to think that any problem we have is our own, and our sole responsibility. Unless we can solve it, we cannot really ever get rid of it and release the burden. Nothing could be further from the truth. There is no reason why the same principle that can be applied to the removal of slower-frequency energies cannot be applied to our everyday problems. We can offer them up to our highest Divine connection, whether it be to God, or to one of the Divine Beings[9] currently gracing the Planet. For example, we can offer our problems up to Mother

Meera, Sai Baba, Ammaji, Meher Baba, or to any other Divine Being with whom we have a clear connection, such as the Christ or the Buddha.

Two things are actually taking place when we give away our problems in this way. The first is that we are actually offering up our experience or difficulty to God, and asking God to deal with it. We are therefore trusting in what God may decide for us. The second effect, and in the longer term a much more profound one, is that we are aligning ourselves, our thoughts, our actions and experiences with that of the Divine. We are making ourselves clear, and are actually laying the foundations for becoming a Divine channel. In this way, we become a vehicle through which Divine Energy can pass, and through which Divine Love and Divine Inspiration can be routed. This indeed is a wonderful way in which we can be of service.

This may sound ambitious, but while it is true that there are many steps on the path to this deeper state of connection, it is also true that one small step leads to another and another and another. When climbing a mountain, if we think constantly of being at the top, we do not concentrate on just going forward, one step after another. In this way, our expectations, and our need to be at the top, make it harder to get there than if we simply put one foot in front of the other, and focus on each small step. After a relatively short period of such simple focus, we find that we have made significant progress. The same rule applies to connecting with the Divine in all of us.

So, by giving everything away to God, we are in fact building up in ourselves a strong alignment with the Divine. There are a number of fairly quick effects resulting from this. The first is that by giving up our problems and leaving them for God to resolve according to Highest Good, we are in fact clearing out slower frequencies and worries, which pull down our vibration. We are also clearing out our mind, which process enables us to feel lighter, and less at the mercy of problems and worries. If we dwell on them less, we feel more content. Since energy follows thought, our whole body system becomes happier.

Please do not interpret what is being said here as an excuse to give up personal responsibility for everything. I do not advocate exchanging a responsible approach for one that says "I have no responsibilities, and therefore it doesn't matter what I do". The laws of karma will still operate! What is advocated is that we remain ever conscious of our responsibilities to ourselves and to others, and seek to live our lives by a code of conduct which is aligned with the Divine and with the Greatest Good. It is in this alignment that we actually perceive, through the proper control and exercise of our heart connection, what is appropriate for any given set of circumstances. I cannot over-emphasise this point. It is not sufficient to absolve ourselves of our responsibilities. It is necessary to align them with the Divine, and it is through this alignment that we will come to understand what is appropriate and proper for each of us at any given time and place.

Connecting with the Group

I now want to discuss group and group consciousness. In days gone by, there was rampant reductionism of thought and deed. By reductionism, I mean that set of principles which seeks to reduce everything to its most basic parts; its lowest common denominator. Reductionism has found its ultimate exposition and expression in concepts such as the 'selfish gene'[10]. With this approach, any group activity or group experience is always, at best, anchored within a selfish perspective, a perspective based on one's own needs above all others. Situations from within each culture can be easily found. For example, it is with a peculiarly British sense of fair play that adults have told children that they shouldn't be selfish, that they should put their elders and betters first. This was often a roundabout and hypocritical way of simply saying "do as I say", and dressing it up as something which it wasn't. This is an important point because in considering the group or the collective, there needs to be a dramatic shift from the basic survivalistic needs of the individual, into the more intuitive expression of the individual within the collective or group.

This shift is significant for several reasons. Firstly, offering up any problems to the Highest Level can also be done through offering them to the group. Any problem shared is a problem significantly reduced. By connecting with the group[11], we have at our disposal, an extraordinary system for connecting with all like-minded light workers. The energy that is brought in by summoning the group is so much greater than any energy that we can bring to bear by ourselves alone. By calling upon the group, we bring in an energy that has as its Source the Divine Intent of the Avataric Will and the Avataric Network[12]. This energy can clear and elevate our frequencies to a higher vibration, and bring us more into tune with the collective consciousness which is demanded by the emergence of the Sixth Root Race.

Swapping Frequencies with the Group

The second important reason for bringing in the group concerns the ability to swap frequencies. We all record frequencies from our experiences, both consciously and subconsciously. By connecting with the group, and opening ourselves out to the group, we can swap these frequencies; mix and match them. So the frequencies that I may register by going to visit ancient sites in Mexico, or in the Philippines, can be experienced and shared by the group. We all engage in this to some degree when we are with other people. When someone comes back with tales of a beach holiday abroad, say in the Caribbean, we can somehow feel, and almost recall, the experience. We are swapping frequencies at one level. By giving away our frequencies to the group as well as receiving from the group, we have access to many more frequencies. It is as if we are small computer terminals that can be plugged into a mainframe. By swapping frequencies, i.e. by plugging into the 'mainframe', we have more information, and access to a much greater ability to act as a collective unit, fuelled (in this instance) by Divine Intent.

Merging with the Group

The third reason for linking into the group is that, with practice, we can open a portal through which we can merge directly with its collective energy. Although we experience our bodies as isolated pieces of biological matter, as solid as any other piece of matter, there is an effective way in which we can learn to merge with the group, and directly connect with other group-members. This is, in one aspect, a precursor to telepathy, but there is a more fundamental reason for this merging: by blending our energies and swapping our frequencies, we can access another person's system, and can connect at a very deep heart level. At this level, we can realise that many of the karmic knots and ties that we may have with that person can be cleared and released, and that we can, in effect, become one, for a period of time. Once we have achieved this, it is always possible to connect with that person.

Achievement of this degree of merging requires a level of trust, love, and clearance of karmic ties which, at first, might seem daunting. However, with practice, it reveals a very fundamental aspect of our nature, namely that we can transmit and receive energy directly from others, without recourse to words. It also makes our systems more flexible in that we are ourselves, while at the same time retaining a collective frequency which is much greater.

The Group and the Sixth Root Race

By connecting with the group we can come to understand the crucial distinction between what our survivalistic tendencies *want*, and what our more intuitive side *requires*. This can mean a radically different approach to life and how we live it. The group connection reveals how we can act for the group and be an integral part of it. The group can become very much a rock, a foundation for our energetic experience in these extremely turbulent times. Acting in concert helps to strip away the needs of the ego, and allows us to live at a different level of experience, infused and connected with light and love.

The group can operate both on the physical planes and on the inner planes. Indeed, it is on the latter that the work of the group is truly done. It can help us to align with our highest accord, with our highest intent, and with the collective infinity of the group. When it is acting under the direction of the Spiritual Hierarchy[13], led by the Avataric Agency, as is beginning to happen, then the group transforms itself into the Mind of One. It can then be said that the Mind of One aspires to the Logos, the Word of the Divine: the Mind of One is created by group intent, and by the fusion of this intent with the Divine. Individual group-members infuse their intent, align themselves with their highest divinity, and allow Divine Love and Power to illuminate their every action and deed. When this happens, the true majesty, beauty, and love of the Divine Plan will be apparent on Earth. Through this alignment, the intent of the Divine Will can be made manifest. This is what has been promised by the Avatar and it is an integral part of the transformation into the Sixth Root Race. It is group alignment with Divine Intent.

Conditional and Unconditional Love

More will be said about the group and the Mind of One, although the foregoing should provide a context for what is to come next. Simply put, this is LOVE. Now we all know, or at least think that we know, what love is. We have experienced it in its many different forms at various times in our lives. However, there are so many different aspects and shades, so many different contrasts of love, that it is often easy to be misled, and to misunderstand what is meant by this term: indeed, different languages have many ways of describing it. At one extreme there is the possessive love which seeks to control, and which, if not satisfied, can easily be turned into hatred. At the other extreme, there is the unconditional love of an Avatar, a Perfect Master or a God-Realised Being[14]. It is between these two extremes that the confusion often arises.

People sometimes say that they love someone and will do anything for them. They seek to climb the steep slope of love to the unconditional peak of purity, from which, they imagine, they can be all things to all people and in everything. In practice, this search for unconditional love is extremely difficult, not necessarily because of our conscious thoughts or actions, but because of many unconscious and karmic connections, which can ensnare us in many different ways. This is not to say that we should not strive for unconditional love; only that to achieve it is much harder and much subtler than we think.

Loving unconditionally means loving without attachment or expectation. If, for example, someone leaves us, then unconditional love would dictate that we accept that, and still love them unconditionally. Even at this point, this definition is wholly inadequate, because it is a mental stipulation or definition, whereas unconditional love can only be felt in the heart, since it is purely of the heart. Above all, the significance of unconditional love for us is this: we may not understand what it truly means nor what it is for us to experience it, but we need to know that whatever God does is unconditional, and is therefore in the best interests of our spiritual evolution. There are no strings attached to God's love. It is pure. Therefore, trusting God to decide what is appropriate is a fundamental acknowledgement that this unconditional love will enable us to move forward in the most appropriate way. This concept takes some thinking about.

To put it another way: in many relationships, problems are encountered because one person is not supplying the love that may be expected from them, or because they are acting selfishly, or because their love is conditional upon what a partner does, or may be expected to do. In circumstances where unconditional love is involved, the situation is different. It is the frequency and the energy of intent within the love vibration that matter, and this is the key to opening our heart more and more. Love cannot be considered from within an intellectual vacuum. This can only be done through experience, in openness, in trust, and in connection with our own deeper divinity. And in struggling to access this deeper divinity, we begin to come to know and connect with a more profound and powerful love; which needs no words, but which irradiates, as an integral part of our vibration. This love forms the core of our existence, our *raison d'être*, and our divinity.

Dimensional Doorways

Our life-span and existence on this Planet are governed by a variety of factors, including our karma and the duration of our contract. While there are many who are very keen to incarnate on Earth at this time, there also appear to be an increasing number of people who wish to escape, and to drop their bodies as soon as possible. This can be attributed to the increasing frequency of the vibration coming into the Planet, but there are other factors involved. Earth acts as a giant portal for incoming and departing souls. The last two great World Wars were major magnets of attraction to these portals. The vortex of energy that was created by the departing souls during the World Wars changed the nature of these portals. As a result, since the 1920s the course of Earth's evolution has radically altered and has coincided with the introduction of new energies through the Spiritual Hierarchy. It was, of course, no accident that this coincided with the Avataric Age and the presence of the Avatar Meher Baba.

While in physical incarnation, His Divine Mission was to map out a new course of evolution for the Planet, different from that which had been previously considered, and to seed and channel these new energies into it.

His Work will resonate for many thousands of years into the future. Its scope and magnitude, and the resultant changes that are taking place on Earth, have not been fully appreciated, and will not be comprehended for many decades.

Renegade DNA

Nor is it generally recognised or understood that the diversity of life on the Planet is being brought into greater unity at this time. This is not merely at the physical level, but also within the higher dimensions, such as the fourth, fifth, and sixth. In practice this means that there is a harmonisation of vibration, particularly at the DNA level. The genetic blueprints for the early Root Races on Earth were originally seeded through the introduction of renegade DNA[15], donated by different life-forms outside of the Planet.

This ancient DNA, which has been significantly tampered with and fragmented through the ages, now needs to be unearthed, reclaimed, and brought to the surface of our genetic expression. The DNA fragmentation which has taken place now needs to be realigned and reharmonised, so that the true genetic heritage of the Sixth Root Race can be brought into being.

Many beings of many different planes and dimensions are now eagerly awaiting the opportunity to connect with the human race, and the other guardian species[16] of the Planet, so that these old DNA fragments can be reactivated. This is an integral part of the transformation into the Sixth Root Race.

> The re-emergence of renegade DNA will enable humankind to carry the higher frequencies implanted within the vehicle of human consciousness and physicality. For example, the new vibrations will harmonise and integrate this renegade DNA within the systems of light workers. When this process is complete, the vibration that will be put out by the collective harmonisation of the renegade DNA will cause a ripple effect, rather greater than that anticipated by the 'hundredth monkey' effect originally observed by your scientists.
>
> This reverberation will further fuse and harmonise the renegade DNA, and open up another portal within your awareness and consciousness. At that time, access will be enabled for higher beings to connect, and to serenade you. The fragmentation of DNA that took place so long ago, and the substantial splintering of these older frequencies, has been at the root of many of humankind's difficulties. It has been partly through the conjunction of the Photon Belt energy, the increasing crescendo of Divine Energy, bolstered through Divine Love, and because this is an Avataric Age that the changes are now taking place.

Atlantean Frequencies

The problems and difficulties that many of us are encountering in raising our vibrations have their roots in the Atlantean age, and the mistakes made at that time. This is not just what took place on the physical planes, but also what arose within our etheric bodies, and more collectively within the astral planes. Much of the energy that was brought through in those times is now being replayed and released. This is one reason for the very 'bumpy ride' that many old Atlanteans are having now. Undoing the past by recreating the future is the key to success in this exercise.

Atlantean practice continues to pervade much of what is taking place today. You can see this in the process of genetic engineering, and in the possibility of the various dramas that could, once more, be played out. Fortunately, the issues are being debated more openly, and the higher vibration that many of us are seeking, in particular the more crystalline vibration, is obviating the likelihood of some of these more extreme forms of genetic engineering. I should add, that much of the concern regarding cloning and similar technologies does not address a central issue. No two individuals who have been produced by cloning could ever be alike, simply because the energy pattern of both creatures would still be different. Nevertheless, the need for neutralising these old Atlantean energies is within us, and is an important part of the process of transformation.

Sharing the New Frequencies

The major key is Divine Intent, and the stepping-down of these frequencies from the Avataric Network into light workers and into the overall planetary population. "Give and you shall receive" is a common saying, and one that has resounded through the ages. It is especially true today in the collective sense. All frequencies that we receive, especially the higher light vibrations, should be shared. This brings us back to the question of merging between different individuals. By sharing these frequencies, it is possible, in an instant, to raise the vibrational frequency of any person, provided they are open to such an experience, whether consciously or subconsciously. When one person acts as a dimensional doorway within his or her own space, it becomes possible for these new dimensional frequencies to come in and be passed on to others. Connecting with these multiple frequencies allows new doorways to open, through which we can begin to become multi-dimensional, i.e. to have an awareness of several places at once, whether this occurs in the physical or the inner planes.

> Significant in this process is the access point. It is essential for any individual to raise his or her frequency so that the purest and highest access note can be achieved. The merging between two individuals of which we have spoken can then arise between the multi-dimensional person and the higher-frequency guests who have chosen to access his or her space. This merging between the physical and the higher dimensions or planes is a key part of the process now happening on your Planet. To understand, through experience, your birthright and your origins within the galaxy is an integral part of the process of coming 'home' within your-selves. How could it be otherwise?

Coming Home

So to understand who we are, where we come from, and what we have to do, is an integral part of a radical awakening process: as we each peel back layer upon layer of information and experiences from our previous incarnations, it will become clearer what 'home' actually means to each of us.

On one level, there will be the recognition that we are immortal, that our physical or human vehicle is on temporary loan to us for this incarnation. We will know that when we drop our bodies we remain conscious and aware, but move up to a different plane of existence. The incarnations that we have experienced are then like beads on a chain, with the chain itself representing the immortality and never-ending experience of our conscious awareness, as it seeks to connect with the God Force that is present within all of us. This is a part of the process of coming home.

But our real home is part of a deeper quest for merging with the Divine; for becoming one with God. So the smaller mergings, if they can be called that, with other beings and other people, both in and out of incarnation, are a continuous preparation for the greater merging with God. It is this ultimate merging that awaits all of us at some time or another.

This concept may seem rather extreme at first, but in truth, the search that each of us has embarked upon can only be understood in terms of the vastness and beauty of Divine awakening and illumination. What else is there? All that we experience during our incarnations on the Planet is, in one sense, an illusion, since the only reality is merging with the Divine. Deeper connection with our true nature, with the Divinity in each of us, will demonstrate the truth of that statement. Once it is understood, nothing can ever be the same again. From a three-dimensional level of consciousness, you will be seen as truly 'bananas'. It is something of a Divine joke.

This is the grace and beauty of the Divine Plan. We work our way through the fog of misunderstanding to realise that our true source and connection are with the Divine Ocean[17]: so for those who believe they are not of this Planet, that is true in one sense. At the same time, we have to operate in the 'here and now'. We need to live and understand our Divine connection. At its simplest, this means recognising that within every moment in the physical, we are to be of service to the Divine. There is no higher service. The only service of note and importance is to the Divine, since it is within us and around all us. God is in everything. So in Divine Service we do service for all things, in all things and of all things. This is the beauty of such work.

Planetary and Human Karma

I now want to move on and look at a number of other issues, or rather in this context, misunderstandings. Much has been written about

Divine cataclysms and disasters leading to the end of the Earth, and life as we know it, and given the 'millennium fever' that is now endemic, it is an appropriate time to consider this. There is an inter-relationship between planetary, solar system, galactic, and collective human karma, as well as our individual karma. As the frequency of the new Root Race increases, and the slower frequencies are spun off, the need to connect with and transmute planetary karma becomes of paramount importance. The tried and trusted methods of transmuting negative karma are usually through illness or accident, often involving a sharp impact of force at a given point. These factors transmute negative karma. The same principal pertains to the Earth. Planetary karma can be transmuted through disease, which can be brought about by famine, flooding, or changing atmospheric conditions. It can also be transmuted through accidents, which in planetary terms translate into earth movements like earthquakes and volcanoes.

The key is the direct relationship and interplay between human and planetary karma. By introducing toxic substances into the environment we are generating karma between ourselves and the Planet: so many of the things that we do have a direct impact on it. If we commit to working with our own karma and how it interacts with Earth, then we can begin to impact planetary karma. The more we fail to clear up or transmute our negative karma, the more likely it is that this karma becomes played out within the framework of planetary illness or movements. The more negative karma which remains, the more likely it is that there is an earth movement. So in a very real sense, responsibility for how the transformation into the Sixth Root Race arises is integral to the intent and will of the human species.

Physical, Astral, and Mental Planes

Another major misconception concerns the physical, astral, and mental planes. Many people do not accept that anything exists outside the physical plane. Those that do accept the presence of an astral or emotional plane, correspondingly do not admit the existence of a mental plane, or if they do, often mistake one for the other. These various forms of experiential nihilism, particularly the rejection of any planes of existence outside of the physical realms, can be very damaging to one's understanding and inner process. By far the greatest amount of change that is currently taking place on the Planet is on the astral planes. It is here that the sum total of the emotional experiences of all the Root Races, from the First to the Fifth, is being played out.

This astral energy is open in that it has direct access to the physical planes. It is also loose or free energy which is 'roaring about' and looking for a place to go. This massive charge is similar to huge ocean waves. Much of it is also of slow frequency, and is therefore attracted to other slow-frequency energy. So whenever we open ourselves up to slower-frequency thoughts, we are also opening ourselves to these enormous waves of astral energy.

The transmutation of this energy is a major task at this time for all light workers, and more will be said of this later. What is equally important to appreciate is that the interplay between physical, astral, and mental karma is a major factor in determining the manner and the current rate of change on the Planet. How we go about working through our karma and handling the slower-frequency energies around us will be reflected in the planetary changes.

When we connect with ourselves, with our heart, anything and everything is possible. The heart is the doorway to the soul, the doorway to the Divine, and thus the doorway to our real home. This is what we seek, and it is our true birthright. Simple, is it not? Everything else is a distraction, for pursuing the goal of connecting ever more deeply with our heart, with our own divinity, is the only activity that will cut through the illusion, or *maya*[18].

Balancing the Heart and the Emotions

We enter the world in a defenceless state. We need our parents to look after us and nurture us. There is a conviction today, in some circles, that our parents never matched or gave what we needed, and that this is the main reason why we are dysfunctional, or angry, or whatever other problem we may have. This is a culture of blaming: in finding excuses, we can blame someone else for the state that we are in.

While there are certainly occasions where our parents may have failed to give us what we needed or required, it is as well to bear in mind that pre-incarnation, it is we who choose our parents, and not the other way round. Their particular strengths and weaknesses are then used as a honing tool for our development and growth. Our interaction with our parents provides a 'cutting edge' for us to grow and evolve. What we do with what we perceive as deficiencies is our business. We can choose either to reflect that which was lacking, and lay the blame on our parents' doorstep, or we can seek to move through the pain, through the barrier of separation, towards love. We can choose to seek a way in which we can integrate what is lacking in us, what may be mirrored in our parents, and what, in many cases, has been put in our path as an experience for growth. This means that if we look to our heart, and feel within our heart at all times, many problems can be removed and dissolved.

You only have to look at those regions where there are wars and outbreaks of continued violence. The cycle continues from one generation to another. It takes tremendous determination and courage to access one's compassion and forgiveness to break out of the karmic cycle. Otherwise nothing changes. More and more people are seeking to do this, to trust their intuition, and move beyond their basic survivalistic need for revenge or to 'balance the books'. This is important, and it is just as applicable to how we look at ourselves and other people. The motto of the Sixth Root Race, in a simplistic fashion, is to care with compassion, but also to care with objectivity and strength and knowledge. Excessive caring leads to an imbalance, just as too little caring does. The relationship between the heart, the emotions, and the head determines the balance in a fundamental way. An excess of emotion or mind may lead to overindulgence. So one of the challenges is to move from the solar plexus, where our emotions are 'located', through to the heart.

There is also a need to move from the head into the heart, which unifies everything: our emotions, our thoughts, and our anxieties. A balanced and deep connection with our heart enables us to care dispassionately; to be more detached, but balanced. From this position the true nature of any connection with another person, or any difficulty in our life, can be approached differently. This is not to rule out the emotions, thoughts, and ideas. It is only to harness their full potential in a more profound way. In this way we are not slaves to our emotions, and we are not ruled by our intellect. But we are *unified* within our heart. Quite a challenge, but a goal that is definitely worth aiming for.

Trust in the Confusion

So where does all this leave us? During this process there will be periods of great confusion, when everything inside will feel upside-down. There will be times when we have no real bearings on who we are, what we are doing, and why we should be doing anything in the first place. It is somewhat analogous to crawling out of the swamp of illusion, the swamp of 'fixity' and deception. This swamp contains frequency 'packets'[19] which have a vested interest in ensuring that each and every one of us remains within it: otherwise these energy packages of slower frequencies will have to find new homes, which is indeed rather tiresome for them. However:

> Even when everything feels as if it is in chaos, in anarchy, there will develop within you a place where you feel calm and stable. It is like becoming used to being in the maelstrom, and realising that it is perfectly alright to be there. And as you become more and more used to it, you will begin to sense a place of balance inside yourself, a solid foundation which can be relied upon during times of great stress and disarray.
>
> Cultivating a trust in this process is particularly important. The epithet "my life is falling apart, I feel awful" can be responded to by saying "sounds great", "no worries", or whatever is appropriate at the time. Although these things are always easier

said than done, once you have faced the maelstrom or inner whirlpool that signifies the transformation of your life into the Divine time-plane that is the Sixth Root Race, you will see that this process has been necessary.

Spiritual dynamite has been required to blast open the fixed doors of perception that have bound us so rigidly to three-dimensional reality. Accepting the chaos, not attempting to change it, going with the flow, are all processes that will help to accelerate the transition. There is no better way, and it may surprise you to see that on the inner planes this process is referred to as being scientific: scientific in its precision, and clinical in its outcome. This is a very different notion of what we normally mean by 'science'. But, in truth, this process of unfolding, of inner opening, is an incredibly precise procedure, and an expression of Divine Intent. It can only be scientific.

Chapter 2 • New Beginnings

The Crystal Skulls

While talking of new beginnings, it is also important that we access and understand aspects of our past. We need not dwell on the past, nor indulge in it; merely to use it as a reference point for our own understanding, and, ultimately, as a release mechanism that will allow us to go forward. For our purposes, the starting point was in Atlantean times. The collective shock-wave and trauma that have echoed through mankind since then, as well as through the representative grouping of higher species endemic to the Planet, are still very much with us, although, the frequency-vibration which is now being emitted from the higher mental planes as a 'keying-in' signature for all light workers is equivalent to, if not higher than, the highest frequency which was present in Atlantean times.

The current collective frequency-signature can be best exemplified in the higher octaves expressed through the artefacts known as crystal skulls. Although there are many of these around, there are only a handful which emit the correct frequency-vibration. This vibration is part of the hierarchical expression of what is manifested through the mental planes. Only these *select* crystal skulls will allow the correct vibrations to come through, and these will hereinafter be referred to as **the Crystal Skull(s)**.

This is especially significant: the frequency that must be accessed needs to be of the highest vibration possible, so that the older frequencies unearthed in Atlantean times can, once and for all, be laid to rest. These new frequencies are of the purest crystalline energy. This may sound odd, but things will become clearer as we progress. The Crystal Skulls express the purest vibrational note, which is in perfect alignment with the Divine Will and the Divine Fire. They therefore represent a 'keying-in' mechanism for all of us.

The Crystal Skulls were seeded into the Planet at the start of the

Atlantean age, some 87,000 years ago. As in all things, there were light and dark skulls[1] present, each with its own specific frequency, and band-width of intent. As the Atlantean period progressed to its awful climax some 10,000 or more years ago, the light crystal skulls were used as specific portals of light and higher frequency-vibrations. These portals now need to be reactivated, so that the crystalline energy that was present in Atlantean times can also be reactivated, and re-utilised in a more direct way. The *most* direct way is through our heart centre: because the frequencies are so high, the keys will only truly become accessible through the intent of unconditional love.

The vortex of Divine Energy that can be made manifest through this crystalline matrix will enable us to come to grips with the new direction that is demanded of us. In essence, this new direction represents the capacity to shift our time lines[2] from the Fifth Root Race to the Sixth Root Race, and the crystalline energy that is accessible through the Crystal Skulls can help us to develop this. It will also represent a turning of the wheel full-circle, from the misdirection of that energy in Atlantean times, through to the appropriate harmonisation of the new frequencies within our hearts and minds in the present day. This process will finally unlock the old Atlantean keys which have held us back on so many different levels, and release us from the burdens of the past. This is one, but by no means the least, of the key aspects of the Crystal Skull frequencies at this time.

> This release of crystalline energy will have a major impact on many levels, first on the mental planes, and subsequently down through the astral planes, where the matrix of old emotions, feelings and energies of the Atlantean age will, once and for all, be brought to the surface for removal and cleansing. This will be a particularly difficult and emotional experience for many of you who were on Earth during those Atlantean times. Many negative thought forms and dark crystalline implants will need to be purged from everyone's system. This process has been

under way for some years, but the intensity will now increase very significantly for many people. This will, in one sense, represent a crossing of the abyss[3], your own personal and collective abyss, and it is important that you remain true to your hearts, and connected with the group at all times.

Although the Crystal Skulls represent one keying-in mechanism, there are others that can be utilised. For example, the Photon Belt is reactivating portals and doorways within multi-dimensional time and space. Its high-frequency photon energy will serve as another springboard for this process.

The Astral Planes and Astral Light

An important factor in understanding these changes is the interrelationship between the different inner planes of existence. The difference between the astral and mental planes is crucial, and more specifically the differences between the various light emanations that are manifest in these planes. Both the astral and mental planes are vast — immeasurably greater than the physical planes of your everyday reality. They can be accessed by going inward into yourselves through one of several doorways, which include the chakras and your subtle bodies. In meditation it is possible to tune into these different planes more specifically, although your awareness may routinely be stationed on different levels within. For example, people who are depressed, anxious, and unhappy are usually positioned on the lower astral planes, where the flux of energies is particularly slow or stagnant. More advanced souls will have many different aspects, positioned through a multitude of levels within the astral and mental planes, and can, with practice, focus their awareness on some of them.

The astral levels house the collective thought forms, both light and dark, of all the Root Races. They are also the focus for many people who have yet to find their way home following physical death. These souls' aspects remain emotionally bound up in the astral levels, and have a need to go back into the light, to the higher planes where they can connect with their higher soul aspects again. Breaking the emotional ties which keep them trapped in the lower planes is difficult, and the emotional distress that these people feel is a major contributing factor to the astral energies.

The astral planes are now opening up in a most significant way. This process has been building over the past few years, and will continue for several more. It is reflected in the major climatic changes and the freak weather conditions being experienced in different parts of your Planet. It is not uncommon to have flash floods, forest fires, and hurricanes in close proximity to one another. Like the weather, the astral-plane drama is formidable.

Picture, if you will, the astral planes as a level where many different frequencies and energies are present, frequencies that span giant octaves of experience and thought. Consider the means by which all of these light and dark frequencies can be mixed into deep and powerful vortices of energy. The analogy to your planetary weather system is extremely apt at this time. Astral storms are like multiple hurricanes and conflicting weather fronts meeting in a morass of different energies. This analogy gives but a scant idea of what is happening on the astral levels at this time. To say that it is turbulent is something of an understatement.

Given that we all have access to the astral levels, how we weather these vortices and fields of energy is of major importance. The waves of energy that are being generated within the tens of thousands of astral sub-planes cannot but have an impact on our physical and mental well-being. The physical symptoms of this drama are too numerous to mention in detail. They include, at one end of the spectrum, feelings of deep tiredness, restlessness, listlessness, and general dissatisfaction. At the other end, there are the more extreme manifestations of deep dis-ease, such as cancer, and the perhaps more disturbing wave of new diseases and epidemics, such as HIV, currently present on the Planet. Many children are also exhibiting disturbing genetic disorders as part of their significant contribution to this cleansing process. All of these symptoms and diseases are part of the physical manifestation of karma, and indicate the necessity for clearing it.

In weathering these astral storms and waves of energy, we must ultimately work our way through the astral planes to the higher mental planes, using our subtle bodies as vehicles of intent. However, this process is difficult. It requires perseverance, and a steady focus within the astral levels on where the way home really lies.

The Mental Planes and Mental Light

As we progress upwards through the higher astral planes, we can eventually connect with the mental planes. These are also known as the causal planes[4], and are, in a very real sense, the point of origin of everything that we find, both on the physical and the astral levels. The mental planes represent the point of initiation, the point of activation, and the point of assimilation. The light-frequencies found within them are a quantum level away from astral light in terms of power, beauty, colour, vibration, and finesse. These vibrations are the corner-stone of our reality, although they remain, for the most part, hidden from all of us. It is this mental light which we now need to access and draw through into the Planet. This is the way home and is the way of the Sixth Root Race — Mental light on Earth.

The mental planes are also much greater than the astral planes, and as mental light pours into the astral layers, the light-frequencies are also activated there, and represent a stepping-down in frequency: in effect, the frequency-vibration initiated in the mental planes is stepped down to a slower frequency in the astral planes, and to an even slower frequency in the physical planes. Thus everything that has its manifestation in the physical planes has, as its point of origin, light from the mental planes.

Consequently, the mental light that is pouring relentlessly out from photon energy and other awesome light sources, including the Spiritual Hierarchy and the Avataric Network, is generating a towering wave of astral sludge, and the release of old frequencies. Thus we see that the only Crystal Skulls of note are those that have direct access to the mental planes and beyond; those that do not have this access being of little value. We can see also that to connect most directly with our source we must focus our gaze on the mental planes, and to connect with them through the astral waste. This is a fundamental challenge for all light workers.

Connecting with Mental Light

The light emanations that manifest downwards from the mental planes are extremely powerful, and yet subtle in their energy. This is something of a paradox to people when they first connect to mental light, since its seemingly cool vibration is at once elusive and yet overpowering. It is necessary to *feel* into mental light; to feel its qualities — the subtlety of its vibration and yet the magnificence of its scope and frequency. We cannot over-emphasise this. Be clear in your connection, and remain strong in your intent to link with mental light. With practice, and through the appropriate group activation and setting, it will become possible to access it.

Since mental light is the initiation point for all thought forms, it is possible, in certain circumstances, to sense it in the form of 'streamers'. These emanate from the higher mental planes, and can appear as ribbons of light trailing down into the millions of sub-planes below. By accessing these ribbons from the planes below, it is possible to trace them up to their point of origin. Above all, though, it is the quintessential *feeling* of mental light which, with practice, will help you to distinguish it from astral light. It is one of those things that you will know with the totality of your being once you have connected with it.

At first it will not be possible for you to hold the vibrational connection with mental light for very long, and it takes a certain combination of concentration and relaxation to keep the frequency within your intent and focus. This is not something that should dismay you, or leave you feeling despondent: accessing mental light directly is something that is earned over many lifetimes of spiritual service, and it requires great dedication and commitment.

The Avataric Age

What you are witnessing today is the culmination of the Atlantean frequency-shifts that were set in motion over 10,000 years ago. The role of the Crystal Skulls is essential as part of this keying-in mechanism, as is the distribution of greater quantities of mental light down to the astral and physical planes. What is also of critical significance today is that you are living in an Avataric Age.

These are defined by the presence of an Avatar, the One who is known as a God-Man. Meher Baba is the Avatar of the Age, and it is His Frequencies that are determining the major ongoing planetary changes in a majestic way. There are, of course, other highly significant Divine Beings gracing Earth today. These include Sai Baba and Mother Meera, who are also often referred to as Avatars, but it was Meher Baba who had the full Avataric attributes, and who has mapped the significant shifts that will be taking place over the next 5,000 years. Meher Baba is, therefore, the true Avatar.

Meher Baba stated that the level of negativity within the planet must be turned around, and drastically shifted from the current level of 75% to the future level of only 25% in the year 2069. This will mark the hundredth anniversary of when He dropped His body. To incarnate in an Avataric Age is extremely fortunate, because any connection with the Avataric Frequency will open new doorways for the individual soul aspect, and for the collective souls on the Planet. It will also lead to new frequency inputs that will, for at least seven generations, echo down the genetic and spiritual lineage of those who come into contact with the Avatar. We would not presume to have, by any means, a full knowledge of the complete work of the Divine Avatar, but it is through His Will, His Love, and His Compassion that humanity will safely and effectively negotiate the crossing of the abyss which yawns before you.

In this context, crossing the abyss signifies a movement from one level of operation, which for most people is either through the solar plexus or the lower centres, up into the heart. When all the old ways of being have been left behind, and the new heart-connection embraced and experientially comprehended, then the abyss will have been crossed. To be in the heart means that one has to act from the heart, but not to act *intellectually* from the heart. This is a point that we shall come back to many times, but from a slightly different perspective each time, so that you can begin to sense what is intended here.

Although your initial connection may be with the *words*, what really matters is the deeper connection with the energy that lies *behind* the words. This is the energy that calls out to the heart, that connects with the heart, and ultimately may open the heart, if only a fraction. This is the call which all light workers across the Planet must respond to, for this is the Truth and this is the Plan. When a sufficient number of your heart centres have become open, and free to receive the Divine message, then the group energy will be fully connected to the Divine, and will send out a giant ripple, a shock wave of light and love around the Planet. This cannot fail to have an impact on those whose heart centres have yet to awaken. This is the Divine Majesty and the Divine Beauty of the Plan.

The Paramatman Light

In one sense it is very difficult to discuss matters which are beyond human knowing and understanding at this time. However, it remains a worthy objective to attempt to give a glimpse of the beauty, the divinity, the all-encompassing knowingness, and the infinite frequencies of light and love that can constitute the Paramatman[5]. Much has been written by many divinely-inspired souls on the subject of the Paramatman, and it is not appropriate that we should try to copy or add to this in a way that does not contribute to these teachings. Instead, we shall focus on connecting with the Paramatman, so that you can begin to sense and experience what this means in terms of your own process, your own evolution, and your own sense of immortality.

The most basic step in initiating a connection with the Paramatman Light is to invoke It whenever you meditate or decide to relax. The more you call It in, the more you will begin to build a bridge to It and the more you will start to connect with It. At first you may feel nothing, but in time you may start to feel slightly different sensations within your body or internal space, which indicate a shift in frequency. This can include a sense of expansion in your aura, an opening in your heart region, or a deeper connection with yourself. All of these experiences are a preparation for connecting with the Paramatman Light.

As you continue to invoke the Paramatman you may sense stronger shifts in the physical. It is important to remember that by Its very nature, Paramatman Light is everywhere, and in everything. Your mind will attempt to control It and define It, but Paramatman Light is not something that can be controlled. Openness and stillness of heart and mind are the best ways of connecting to It. At the same time, since It cannot be defined, it is not appropriate to think of It in terms of light or colours or frequencies. The Paramatman Light will appear in Its own way to you at the appropriate time, and by continually invoking Its Presence you are building a bridge to the Divine.

Paramatman Light is the highest frequency of light that we can access on the physical planes. It is the Divine Light; the light which passeth all understanding and all knowledge. Paramatman Light simply *is*. If we seek to connect with It, then our physical and subtle bodies will be inspired and saturated by It, saturated to the point where we can handle no more. By invoking the Paramatman Light, we are connecting with our highest self, with our Divine self, with the divinity which is in all of us, irrespective of who we are and what we have done in the past. This is the gift that is being seeded into the Planet, and which should be accepted with all our hearts and minds.

Whenever we visit a Divine Being, an Avatar, or a Perfect Master, we can connect directly with the Paramatman Light. Those who have been fortunate enough to visit Mother Meera in Germany or Sai Baba in India can receive a direct infusion of the Paramatman, through Their Divine Love. In particular, Mother Meera specialises in bringing down the Paramatman Light into the Planet. This is a gift that is unique to us. It has never happened in this way before, and is unlikely to occur in this manner ever again.

While we may not be able to sense the presence of the Paramatman, or to connect with it directly, a visit to Mother Meera or Sai Baba will always bring about a change in our consciousness and a change in our karmic 'flavour'. This is a result of the direct effects of the Paramatman Light entering our physical vehicles. The more we ask for, the more we can handle, then the more we will be given. There is no limit to the Divine. So as we invoke, and the key here is to *invoke* the Paramatman, then we may receive as much as we can handle, both physically and at all other levels. To receive the Paramatman Light in this way is an extraordinary gift, and one reason why so many souls are keen to incarnate on Earth.

The Paramatman has been on Earth in many different guises over many ages. What is unique today is that It is being poured directly into the Planet without any stepping-down of Its frequency through intermediate energy sources.

Mindfulness and the Mental Planes

To further what has been said about the different plane levels and the Paramatman Light, it is important to appreciate the connection with the mental planes. This is not a reference to our higher mental faculties in the normal sense of 'mental', but to an ongoing process of building a strong and vibrant connection to the mental planes and mental light.

This is a particularly interesting journey, and one of which this channel has some experience. The first step is to be able to go inside, to meditate, to loosen the shackles of your mind, and the thoughts of everyday activities, such as where the laundry has been put, or what you forgot to do. While these thoughts will pop up from time to time, it is as well to focus within, on your own light. Connecting with your own light source is rather like peeling away the layers of an onion, and setting up an initial link is relatively simple. It involves focussing ever more deeply in meditation. Once in a meditative state, begin by feeling intuitively within the space around you to where you sense that there may be a source of light. This source can be from any direction within your awareness. You should also ask to connect intuitively with the Divine Light, the Paramatman Light, for joining with the highest Source of light is the starting-point. It is your awareness which will ride upon this wave of light as it begins to build a bridge to the different levels within yourself. This is not a linear process. It is an ever-dynamic multidimensional process of moving through various access points within yourself into different dimensional experiences. Again, trust is the key.

While there may be times when you cannot intuitively feel anything, at other times it may be clear. Use these times of clarity as reference points. As your connection grows stronger, so your light source becomes more vibrant. This source is a signpost to your own inner divinity. Focusing and meditating on the location of this source, and developing ways to access it more easily, will help to build up the link.

It is this interaction with the highest frequencies of light that will help you to weather the astral levels, and to retain a fixed and secure reference point inside yourself, a point which cannot be moved by any external force.

Extra-Terrestrial Frequencies

Much has also been written about extra-terrestrial frequencies entering the Earth at this time. The most significant event in recent years was the opening of a dimensional doorway in April 1997, that gives access to a number of new extra-terrestrial frequencies emanating from the mental planes. This last aspect is particularly important, because many people have become more obsessed with the lower-frequency extra-terrestrial thought forms, such as the 'greys'[6]. The time has come to 'up' the frequency, and to connect with your extra-terrestrial brothers and sisters, who manifest the higher frequencies of love and light. This will represent a coming home in many ways, not just on a planetary level, but also on a galactic level. Those of you who have experienced a broad range of extra-terrestrial past lives will find this new opening deeply moving and extremely powerful. The same will also be true for your extra-terrestrial brothers and sisters, although the manner in which this will manifest itself to them will be different, because they do not have the same emotional base as the human species.

It is essential to remember during this 'coming home' that the physical appearances of your extra-terrestrial friends will be significantly different from your own, and we do mean *significantly* different. There will be a real need to move away from the anthropomorphic view of humanoid species populating the stars, and to open your hearts to the new vibrations that are coming through. This is all part of the Sixth Root Race emergence and manifestation. The lessons that you can learn, and the training you will receive in the merging with your physical brothers and sisters on Earth will keep you in good stead with the merging that needs to take place with your galactic brethren. Again, the heart connection is the key, because physical appearances can be deceptive. Gauging the communication through the heart will allow you to connect, and to move through any old fear patterns and structures that may hold you back.

The importance of this process cannot be over-emphasised. Your extra-terrestrial brothers and sisters will be bringing through higher-frequency energies that will be a seeding mechanism for accessing higher mental frequencies, and furthermore will link into the frequencies expressed by the Crystal Skulls. When you link with these higher frequencies, two things can happen. First, there is a tremendous downloading of information from your extra-terrestrial counterparts, and also a reciprocal transmission from you to them, rather like a mutual admiration society in terms of swapping frequencies.

The second, and possibly more significant, series of events will centre on the further realignment of your DNA structure to accommodate the new extra-terrestrial frequencies. This will involve an elongation of the frequency signal that can be emitted by your DNA. As has been mentioned before, DNA is a frequency-transmitter at its most basic level. It receives, transmits, and stores data. The longer your DNA[7], the greater the frequencies that can be accommodated within your physical space. Ultimately, this facilitates the merging process, so the two events tend to go hand-in-hand: downloading and transmission of information, accompanied by DNA realignment and frequency harmonisation.

Accessing Extra-Terrestrial Frequencies

Different people will have access to different frequencies or extra-terrestrial connections, depending upon past-life connections.

These new linkages will open up a dialogue that will bring through to you the knowledge and understanding gained by the Star People over millennia. This information is precious, and it will be communicated in a wide variety of ways: painting, music, writing, singing, science, and love, to name but a few. If you begin to manifest some of these extra-terrestrial connections, then do not *expect* anything. The medium through which you will eventually choose to express these frequencies will suit your old connections most appropriately, and these may be rather different from your current expectations.

Crystal singers of old will have a further chance to refine their vocal chords, and to bring through the ancient Divine Frequencies. In many ways, this will be a bringing-together of a multitude of ancient and beloved frequencies from the past. The best of the old Root Races will be brought through alongside the new planetary frequencies. This is a momentous and extremely exciting process, and it is another reason why your star-brothers and sisters are so excited by the prospect of connecting with you.

DNA and Extra-Terrestrial Frequencies

Another cause of the excitement in the extra-terrestrial realms concerns the donated DNA present on this Planet. The basic DNA body-plans[8] that are represented through the animal, plant, and mineral structures, have been donated from other planetary systems in many different ways. The donated DNA has come from numerous planets and races, and the transition that is now occurring is part of a realignment which requires the removal of virulent sections of DNA which inhibit the harmonisation of the ancient DNA. This process also requires a recognition that we have, at some time in the past, incarnated through these ancient body-plans.

The physical shells of many DNA frequencies are also being realigned, so that the planetary changes are not just affecting human beings, but all life on the Planet, as it moves from one frequency-setting to a much higher one. The reconnection of the Star People with these different frequency-settings, which are present in all planetary life-forms, is part of this process.

Amplifying Planetary and Stellar Frequencies

The frequency-vibrations that are now entering the Planet are elevating the harmonic resonance of the interplanetary connections being made between Earth and neighbouring planets such as Sirius, Alcyone, and Dagar. The higher resonance will further amplify the energies between these and other neighbouring planets. Consequently, the purity of the crystalline frequency-vibration that is being brought in will carry a combination of these planetary and stellar frequencies, the conjunction of which, combined with the intensity and span of the vibrations, will further enhance the collective vibration emergent on Earth. This will be both a collective vibration within human minds and the Mind of One, and the establishment of a collective energy-wave between Earth inhabitants and the star-brothers and sisters from your neighbouring planets. The diversity and beauty of these frequencies will be beyond your wildest imagination. The final touches to this initiation sequence were established in March 1999. It is now a case of 'watch this space'.

For many light workers there will be some initial difficulties in adapting to these new, resonant harmonic frequencies. It will necessitate an expansion of the scope of your frequencies to accommodate the new array of vibrations. Equally importantly, they will require good earthing techniques, based on a sound practice and discipline, geared to acquiring and anchoring them into the Planet. This alone will prove a mighty challenge for many of you.

Removing Slower Extra-Terrestrial Frequencies,
and Becoming Multi-Dimensional

> An array of new doorways will be opened to many different dimensions and levels of light. As mentioned previously, this will necessitate the removal of old, slower frequencies from your systems. For example, old extra-terrestrial or ET implants and slow-frequency transmitting devices will need to be disposed of. For the most part this will involve a cleansing of your etheric bodies, in conjunction with a clearing of the various astral levels: just as you have experienced light and dark incarnations in human form, so it is with your extra-terrestrial heritage. Remain connected, and at all times offer up to the light whatever arises for you.

Many surprises are in store for us. Acknowledging and connecting with our older reptilian[9] aspects will be a shock for some, but they form an important part of the overall process. A clearer understanding of the nature of our multi-dimensional self, and what it means to be multi-dimensional should emerge. We are, in a sense, already multi-dimensional, because we are saturated with so many incoming frequencies, on all the levels that we inhabit. This is what is meant by being multi-dimensional, and understanding it can take us much deeper into ourselves. As the veil of illusion is slowly lifted from our consciousness, we can begin to gain a deeper understanding of multi-dimensional reality. In its turn, this deeper understanding begins to give meaning to the collapsing of time, and to an appreciation of our past, present, and future lives.

In one respect, this amounts to nothing more than lifting the veil on the two main frequencies that govern reincarnation. The first of these is time, and the second comprises death and rebirth. These twin frequencies are combined with a healthy dose of spiritual amnesia: when we reincarnate, we have no recollection of who we are, and where we have been. It is only through a progressive process of re-awakening that we can begin to remember who we are. This spiritual amnesia will be rudely dispelled in the new Root Race. There will occur in our psyche an awakening of such magnitude that the vistas of past, present, and future will begin to come together in a unique and inspiring fashion.

Again, the key to negotiating this process lies in our managing our expectations: or rather, in not managing them, in the sense that it is always better to have no expectations. So if as you read this you begin to establish an expectation of what it all means and how you will experience it, you are setting up a vibration which may dominate, and preclude other vibrations from coming in. This vibration, or thought form, will then inhibit, to a greater or lesser extent, the full tapestry of your experience; the full vista of possibilities, either realised or unrealised. The cultivation of an attitude of no expectation whatsoever is, therefore, an important part of this process.

Avataric Chants

Cultivating an attitude of no expectations is not easy, and it requires patience, honesty, and awareness at all times. The use of various Avataric chants can be very beneficial. Such chants help to clear the mind of any unnecessary thoughts or ideas, and they refine both frequency and mental attitude, so that the mind will have more in common with a laser than with a wet blanket, the latter being the operative word for where most of your mental frequencies reside. The Avataric chants can be focused on a number of Divine Beings, such as Meher Baba, Mother Meera, Sai Baba and the Christ. The chants are as follows: *Meher Baba* for Meher Baba, *Meera Ma* for Mother Meera, *Om Sai Ram* for Sai Baba, and *Lord Jesus* for Jesus Christ. Repeating each of these chants individually or collectively will help you to connect more directly with these Divine Beings and with your inner essence, and to remove the external mind-manifestations which can often waylay you.

The beauty of this unfolding will be unparalleled on this Planet, and will manifest itself to each of you in different ways, according to your frequency-vibration, the amount of energy that your system can hold, and the courage and commitment that you have.

Quantum Connections with the Divine

The importance of connecting with your Divinity, your highest access point, cannot be over-emphasised. Recognising that the Divine is within you is the first critical step in this process. For many people, this appears an insurmountable goal. Your past experiences, the countless times that you have crash-landed[10] on to the Planet, the multiple fragmentations of your past life-aspects, have all led to a severing of the knowledge which is yours by birthright. The knowledge is buried so deep within you that accessing it, even believing in it in the first instance, is extremely difficult, and requires a great deal of trust.

There are those who believe that any notion of Divinity is out of the question in the first place. This is because the intellectual constraints imposed by our minds as a result of a rigorous education in logic and linguistics, science and so on, have all but severed the intuitive link that we all have with the Divine within us. To move from this position of atheism or agnosticism is difficult, and may, to some, seem impossible. Yet it will happen, for many people.

The breathtaking speed with which their grounded perceptions will be shattered, the way in which the veils of illusion will be stripped away, will stun their minds into submission and into silence. For it is truly in silence that the knot of karma or the cord of untruth can be severed within them, so as to allow the Divine Spark of intuition to shine forth in love and light.

Acknowledging the harmonics of your own intuition, the harmonics of your divinity, and the harmonics of your own frequencies, is about following your true journey home: a journey home into your essence, your core, your own healing, and your own inner perceptions. When you are so far removed from it, it is easy to believe that you have no real home — that no such place exists. It is easy to believe that what is presented to you in the cold stark unreality of your myths and legends is untrue, that the world you live in is mechanical, and that everything around you can be reduced to the lowest common denominator. Yet all of this has been shown to be untrue: by your modern physics, by quantum mechanics, and its deeper analysis of the world around you. You may intellectually understand modern physics, but it is quite another matter to accept that what is stated *intellectually* actually resonates and reverberates within the very fibre of your being.

For example, you can experience being in two places at once, and your mind can travel vast distances in an instant. None of this is prohibited by modern physics. Quantum theory accepts that an aspect of yourself can be present in two places at once. It is just that you need to trust your own impressions in these experiences. The quantum aspects of physics can give you the clues for unlocking your own divinity. For those of you who are wedded to logic, science, and objectivity, might it not be an interesting experiment to radicalise this view, this objectivity, and to see what it means to experience the ideas of relative space, relative time, and relative motion? Why not try to experience, in your own essence, the subtle dimensions of the body? Certainly not everything that is invisible is unreal. Physics teaches this. The same applies to your everyday experience. Just because you cannot experience an event in the normal, visual way does not mean that it does not exist. It is rather like extending your senses or your experiences into a different realm of being. This new realm is all about being with the instantaneous, and being subtly connected with everything around you at many different levels. This approach is a key, a frequency which can help you to unlock your own divinity.

Opening to the Inner Divinity

Once you have an inkling that there is something more to connect with, something more to be unlocked, why should you discount the notion of your own divinity, as opposed to some other form of experience, such as existentialism[11]? Given the multiplicity of possible experiences, and the *interpretation* of such experiences, ranging from mechanistic[12] to holistic[13], from dadaist[14] to vedantic[15], from conceptual[16] to holographic[17], and so on, there is no reason to exclude a Divine Aspect, a Divine Presence within you. Once you give some credence to this basic position, even if it is just for the sake of it, then you will have taken a step to admitting the possibility of different levels within yourself. There are many things that remain difficult to explain experientially: where does love come from? Where does hatred come from? Where does fear come from? Where does anger come from? These are all frequencies, and they give a clue as to your versatility and divinity. It is not that these frequencies should be belittled or ignored, it is that you express all aspects of divinity within you, automatically. This is what matters.

All of this refers to a perceptual shift at one level. But there is something else, something much more profound and germane. If you can accept that there is an aspect of the Divine within you, then there is a point to accepting yourself as you are. This acceptance is not about judging yourself. It is about recognising that your own inner core, your own inner vibration, has a divinity to it: a Divine spark of love and light. How much of this spark of light and love you absorb into yourself, is entirely up to you. All you have to do is to invite it. Once you have made that quantum leap — a distance that is, all at once, so small, so huge in terms of its ramifications — then it can be said that one abyss within yourself has been crossed. You may also find that this spark of light and love rapidly becomes a torrent, and ultimately an avalanche.

To be able to invoke, to ask to be shown your own divinity and your own true nature, is profoundly liberating and to know that this is all just a thought away, and to understand the distance that such a thought, request, or invocation can take you, is awesome. You need *emotion* to back up this invocation, because the more you mean it, the more it will happen. Here is another pointer: why not really mean it for the sake of it? You have nothing to lose. There are no limits in this, because these 'quantums' or jumps are there for the taking. Just as sub-atomic or quantum physicists know about the differences between the position of a particle and its momentum[18], so you can experience the quantum difference between being connected or not connected to your own divinity. The choice is yours. There are many layers to these quantum connections, and what has been described here barely scratches the surface.

The Divine Within Us

The words 'the Divine within us' have an echo that goes far beyond our knowing. This notion of our own divinity is central to the Sixth Root Race as it forms, and emerges from the collective frequency and thought form that are being constructed by light workers on the Planet. It is important to be aware that this divinity is not an ego-orientated 'I am so wonderful and so divine, that I am better than anybody else'. It is not something that comes from the mind. It has to come from the heart, to be a natural outflowing and inflowing of the heart, like every breath that we take in and out. It is as natural as that.

Once you recognise this divinity, it will be clear that everything else around you is divine, including other people, races, creeds, and nationalities. There is no separation or elevation in this, and there is no change or discrimination imposed by the mind. It is just a deep acknowledgement that we are all Divine Beings, rooted and grounded on Earth, and that expressing our divinity within the human, physical form is perfectly natural. There is no separation within this divinity; it simply *is* — a wholeness or oneness, if you like. The same is true of our connection with the animal and plant kingdoms. There is divinity in all animals and plants, and even minerals, not least because our own evolutionary path has taken on these forms as expressions of our experiences. We have evolved upwards through the mineral, plant, and animal kingdoms, not in a Darwinian[19] sense, but in the sense that our own soul evolution has taken on forms within these kingdoms, and moved up through them. So we are all interconnected in this way. The Divine Spark is in everything.

This is not easy to understand, nor even, initially, to believe. It is only through uncovering our own expression of divinity, through coming to terms with who we really are, that we can begin to absorb the wonder of these truths. So if you or I can come to a point where we *feel* (not intellectually understand or conceptualise) the divinity within us, then this *feeling* also shows the way, or sparks the intuitive realisation, that everything else around has its own divinity. This truth is of crucial significance. It will be a fundamental anchor-point for the changes that will occur over the next sixty years.

> In recognising your own divinity, you can actually begin to see and feel your own immortality. This is not the rather absurd notion of trying to live for thousands of years, or through putting your body into cryopreservation in the hope that you will be woken up in several hundred years' time, when there may be a cure for a fatal disease which currently afflicts you. Rather, it is an acknowledgement that through your own divinity, there is a part of you which survives your physical-plane death, a part which is the one true connection with your own source and your own soul, and which is but an aspect or manifestation of God, the Divine. This is what matters. This is what is meant by finding out *who* you really are and *what* you really are. The local form or vehicle which you take is incidental. It is the immortal aspect, the Divine aspect within you, which matters. If you look

at the world you inhabit from this deep perspective, or in a true connection with yourself, then everything begins to look very, very different.

So feel this Divine connection within your heart, within your whole body, and even within your mind, until it becomes an everyday reality, a vibrant reality which can harness your true potential.

The Divine and the Infinite

This sense of your own divinity is a platform from which you can begin to connect much more deeply with other divine beings. In accessing this connection you may begin to feel that there is an unconditionality, a beauty, and a *heart* in this. Imagine the aeons that you have existed, from the time when you initially became separate from God. From the beginning, when the breath of the Creator[20] moved across His Awareness, and spawned a new Awareness, a separate Awareness, right through to the present time, when you inhabit your present vehicle. This is something that is truly awesome. Not because of who you are now, but because of what you are in reality, in an immortal sense. The local customs are just that, very local, but the majesty and divinity in the hundreds and thousands of lives that have been played out by your soul aspect are truly magnificent and Divine. This is what you need to connect to. It rather puts things into perspective.

Although you may not believe it, you have connected with this divinity within yourself before. It is just that you have forgotten about it. In each life, you are obliged to go through this process of 'instant recall'; although for some the recall is not so instant. But this recall, this acknowledgement that you have a divine connection, and that you have connected with it before, is a preparation for what is to come.

To summarise, much of what has been described is similar

to the initial ascent to base camp, prior to climbing Mount Everest. It is hard but necessary groundwork for the ascent in frequencies that is to come. In simple terms, this means that you can connect with your heart, feel the divinity within you, have a sense of your own immortality, truth, and oneness. This idea may in itself seem wondrous to you, but it is no more than the tip of the iceberg. The space that your heart occupies within your physical vehicle and your subtler bodies is but a beginning. As your heart becomes bigger (and in physical terms we can refer to this as your heart chakra), the capacity to handle and hold the Divine Light, the Paramatman Light, is increased. Since the Paramatman Light is the Light that passeth all understanding and all knowing, it is also true that your conception of what your heart can hold and feel is limited only by — your conception!

In connecting with the Infinite, by definition nothing is finite. In connecting with and recognising your own divinity, please understand that this connection is in itself unfathomable, infinite, and majestic in its scope. There are no words that can describe it. It can only be experienced. As you begin to invoke the Divine Light into your heart, you are connecting directly with God the Divine, Who is limitless.

The Journey into the Heart

This journey into your heart will show you that there are many kinds of love; but of all of them, the most deep, compelling, compassionate, and loving form is Divine Love. Nothing can ever surpass It, because It and the Paramatman Light come from the Source, the Highest of the High, and are the One True Frequency of Love. All others are merely stepped down into physical matter in various ways. Conditional love is a stepping-down into physical matter of love frequencies, and in the stepping-down, they are diluted.

Incarnation and the Human Experience

The human experience is to anchor these frequencies into our heart, while giving them expression and intent on the physical planes. It is as if we are allowed to play with them. So what happens if I incarnate with someone with whom I have negative karma? At the same time I am given, as a frequency through my heart connection, the capacity to love this person very deeply. Perhaps over many lifetimes, the ultimate outcome will be that the higher frequencies of Divine Intent, of Divine Love, will burn away this karma. All that will remain will be a clear understanding of what love is in a certain context. And so it is that we go on experimenting with many different people whom we have met before, with a myriad of love vibrations. These situations can be presented within the family, within a relationship, within a work environment, and so on. This is what the process of incarnating and understanding our love, and our capacity to love, is all about. Ultimately it will *always* lead us to Divine Love, because this is the highest frequency. It is the frequency which beckons us across the mists of time, and through the veils of various incarnations. This is truth, beauty, and part of the Divine Plan.

It is as if the mixture of love and light that is being poured into the heart is being altered, upgraded, realigned, and readjusted. Just as our heart has to adjust, to expand enormously, so it is that everything else within our physical vehicle has to follow suit. Our glandular systems, our endocrine systems, our central nervous system patterns, our growth and digestive systems, all follow the calling of our heart. Sri Aurobindo[21] talked about one single cell in the body becoming truly divine, and this is the blueprint and the ideology of the Sixth Root Race. Put simply, it is that each and every cell of our body can be bathed in Divine Paramatman Light and that this Light will so raise our frequency-vibration that we shall be able, more fully, to live the Divine life on the Planet.

This means that our notion of our own divinity will be so drastically changed, radicalised, modified, that our conception of the Divine today, will have been superseded by what we think, or rather feel it to be in five years time, in ten years time, and so on. It is ever-changing as the frequencies within our hearts increase, so the connection with our own divinity increases, and our capacity to love, and to be compassionate increases. The grand adventure, the grand experiment, is to transform humankind's sense of its own divinity into something totally different from what has gone before. This new divinity will be complete and replete in its unconditionality. This is a beautiful and awe-inspiring chapter in our evolution and our spiritual development.

Heaven on Earth

As we connect with the Divine Light and invite the Paramatman into our space more and more, so our vibration increases, so our sense of the Divine will increase, and so will the ramifications or expressions of this divinity increase one-hundred-fold or more, although in truth it is meaningless to put numbers on it, because the depth of expression becomes ever deeper. The Sixth Root Race is Heaven on Earth. Once again, we have to *feel* into what is being said. Not to understand it intellectually, but to *feel* with our heart into the energy behind the words. Only in this way, shall we gain an understanding of what is meant by connecting more deeply with our own divinity, and coming into the divinity that is demanded by the Sixth Root Race.

The grand experiment thus demands that we connect with our own divinity as it is currently expressed. It demands that we invoke from within ourselves the capacity to connect more intensely with our own divinity. In this process of invocation, we shall transform our deep connection with our own divinity into something much more profound, intense, and aligned with the Divine. Once we have done this, we must continue to invoke our divinity throughout our physical and our subtler systems, until we feel we can absorb no more. Even then we must continue to invoke, for the Divine, in truth, knows no boundaries. This invocation is a staircase which will lead us to the realignment of our frequencies with those of the Sixth Root Race. We are completely transforming our connection with the Divine in every way and sense, in each and every cell, and throughout every subtle body, to a deeper and deeper level. This connection can only be known through experience, and through the true frequencies of light and love. We are all participating in a grand experiment of connecting, ever more deeply, with Divine Love.

Chapter 3 • The Sixth Root Race

Transforming into the Sixth Root Race

As your frequencies ascend, you will begin to shift your time-line more dramatically into that of the Sixth Root Race. In one respect, this is a thought form, and it is only through a sufficient number of light workers invoking it into their space, that the promised transformation can take place. What makes this experiment unique is that the transformation is happening during the course of your lives in this incarnation. This does not mean that it will be completed during your lifetime, since this will take many years. Rather, it is that you are retaining and evolving your physical form during this transformation, as opposed to dropping one body-form at the end of one Root Race, and replacing it with an entirely different one at the initiation of the succeeding Root Race. This means that the current evolution will place considerable stress on your physical vehicles. Clear and consistent practice in all aspects of your spiritual and physical life are essential to this transformation.

We have already spoken of some of the key features: for example, connecting with your own divinity, and holding the frequency-note that is being transmitted in earnest from the mental planes. You must invoke the Paramatman Light on a constant and continued basis, daily if possible. This is what the Divine Mother, Mother Meera, does. She feeds into the Planet a never-ending stream of mental light for you to connect with and absorb. This in itself is a great act of beauty and divinity.

You also need to experience this connection with mental light and the mental planes in a physical way. You have to bring the thought form into reality in a very concrete way, so that you can experience the presence of mental light within your own space. How can you do this, and how will you know that you have achieved it?

The first step is to invoke constantly the Paramatman Light. The second step is to ask to be as open as possible to receive It, so that your own preconceptions of what is and what is not possible may bypass your mind. This approach will help to remove any constraints placed by your mind on the amount of light you can potentially receive. This is of particular importance. The third step requires that you seek and connect with the Divine Mother, Mother Meera, as often as possible. This does not necessarily mean going to Germany to receive Her Divine Darshan in person (although visiting Her obviously helps to access Her Physical Appearance within the mind's eye, which builds a bridge to Her on an everyday basis). A connection with the Divine Mother can be cultivated on the inner planes. As in your meditations you invoke according to Highest Good[1], you will in effect be building a bridge to Her: no Avatar or Perfect Master can refuse or ignore a call from a truly devoted disciple.

Connecting with the Divine Mother

Try to visualise the Divine Mother's space in your mind's eye as an area of beautiful exquisite blue light, or whatever frequency comes to you intuitively. Once you connect with Her Divinity, you will start to feel Her frequency — gently at first, and then more powerfully as your connection is stepped-up in speed and strength. You will never be given more than you can handle, since the system[2] always works in perfection, although your minds may not always perceive this to be the case. As in your heart you build this bridge to the Divine Mother, you will begin to feel the benefits of the Paramatman Light. Feel in your heart for Her Beauty, Her Divinity, and Her Love. These are second to none, and can help you to see and feel the possibility of your transformation in a very tangible and personal way. This is an unprecedented opportunity for your soul aspect at this time, so take it, rejoice in it, and feel free to ask for more. The supply is never-ending. Allow this light also to connect with your family and friends. Since you operate on an increasingly collective basis now, and will do so more and more, invoking this light for others has great value.

As your vibration increases, those around you may at first seek to reject or negate it. This is a natural response to an extremely powerful energy source and light frequency. There is usually a deep residual fear within people that they might not be able to handle the light and love, or that at some level they are unworthy of such Divine blessings. Nothing could be further from the truth. Everyone has a right to ask to be connected to the Divine Mother, and through Her to find a deeper communication with their own heart and with those around them.

The Spectrum of Sixth Root Race Frequencies

In stepping up the frequencies of your physical, astral, and mental bodies, you are bringing in the Sixth Root Race frequency, which is at one and the same time both crystalline and earthy. It is a frequency that unifies and accommodates the planetary vibrations as expressed through different aspects of light on the Planet. This includes the dolphin energies, the fairy, gnome, and goblin energies, and many, many more. The essence of the Sixth Root Race is about allowing all life-forms to turn towards the light in an unprecedented way, and it includes all of these energies. No being or energy is excluded: each one has a choice to connect with the new vibration, since every being has a divine right to connect with the light, and with Divine Love.

During the transition, the choices put before every living being will allow a segregation of energies. These choices will include connecting with the new frequencies, and, ultimately, whether or not to connect as deeply as possible with the Sixth Root Race thought form. It is clear that some groups of species have chosen not to connect with it at this time. This is their choice, and as some of these organisms leave the Planet, they will be replaced by other groups of organisms that are seeking to connect with the new thought forms and energies.

This is not something to get emotionally attached to (as some of you have done) for it is nothing more than a succession, alteration of frequencies, which is demanded by the planetary changes at this time. Your fears and worries over BSE[3] are but one example of this. The domestic cattle that have served humanity for so long have decided, in some areas, to move into a different dimension, a different expression of life. That is their choice, and it must be respected. The presence of BSE is but an external aspect of this transition. For some, this viewpoint will be particularly difficult to understand, although this will change. Similar situations have arisen in the past, as with mass extinctions[4], or the destruction of previous Root Races. In fact, the decimation of past races and civilisations provides a clear example of such events.

However, the wheel turns, and many new races and frequencies are now extremely eager to enter the Planet. The old Native Americans, many of whom have served us on the inner planes, are keen to incarnate, and to bring their own brand of wisdom and depth to the Sixth Root Race frequencies. Their earthiness, their deep understanding of the Earth are clear examples of the wide spectrum of frequencies. We shall return to this theme further on.

Recapitulation of the Root Races

In the succession of plant, mineral, and animal life that is being played out on this Planet, it is important to understand the significance for humanity. The old systems and the old practices of selfish expression, of survivalistic[5] tendencies, have to go. They are unacceptable within the new frequencies, which is why transformation and release of the past are so important. The emerging connection to your heart, the guidance from the heart, and the accessing of the new frequencies through your heart, will require a deep trust and intuition that cannot develop in the context of survivalistic tendencies. This is why the group dynamic, the collective intelligence, and the collective thought form that are being established, are so essential. It is critical that you let go of these older survivalistic frequencies, and embrace the new rays of excellence that are entering the Planet.

Ironically, it will be a matter of survival for you to move from your solar plexus into your heart. As you let go of your survivalistic tendencies, the final abyss that you must cross within yourselves requires that you make this shift as a matter of urgency. This is something which can only be *done*: it cannot be intellectualised. This is the paradox that will be presented to many of you. A key to the path through this transition is to begin to trust your heart. Your heart will tell you what you need to do, and what you need to experience, and will indicate whether or not you are in the right place at the right time, or in the wrong place at the right time, or whatever. Cultivate this keying-in of your intuition through your heart, and trust it.

So part of the preparation is a cultivation of this intuitive input. It will sit side-by-side with your emerging divinity, love, and compassion.

Telepathic Communication

As the Fifth Root Race draws to a close, it is as well to consider what it has meant to us. What does the past represent, and what, in our dreams, should the future represent? As the time lines disintegrate, the possibilities for new beginnings and new futures are staggering. What would it be like, for example, to live in multi-dimensional reality, where we can connect with our group and our loved-ones in a telepathic way? We already do this empathetically, so why not telepathically? Similarly, consider the beauty and depth of telepathic connections with other beings; Divine Beings, animals, plants, minerals, stones, and all manner of different life-forms, both on and off the Planet. The possibilities for communication, for communing and connecting with these different life-forms are manifold.

Communication has to be a two-way thing and we can be sure that the desire to communicate is very powerful in non-human forms, or 'the other side'. Plants, animals, and minerals are all keen to communicate with human beings. The endless possibilities for opening up and communicating in this new way are extremely beautiful, and we are told that experiencing these potentials will take our breath away. Sceptics may argue that such communication is pointless. However, put simply, the *point* is that there is intelligence in *all* of life; what we may call Divine Intelligence. And as we open and communicate with these different Divine Intelligences, so we become increasingly illuminated, and more closely aligned with our own Divine Intelligence. This is truly Heaven on Earth.

A different way of looking at this is in the context of evolution. In our own evolutionary march, we have connected with an ever-broadening array of life-forms. We shall begin to have a deeper connection with what our journey represents, and how we have built up such a diverse series of frequencies. To have experienced being a wild grass in a glade, or the collective aspirations and frequencies of many different species in their own specific form of intelligence, is incredibly beautiful. It also represents a coming-together, a merging, in a new and fundamental way. This is what is so vital about opening up to these new forms of communication within our internal and external spaces.

Planetary Frequency-Holders

For those of you who are known as planetary frequency-holders[6], this will be an inspirational experience, and one that you will have awaited over many millennia. The flexibility that will be demanded of your DNA substance will be enormous, but as you raise your vibration, and remove any blockages, you will begin to consider, in a rather different way, the true meaning of the expression 'Unity through Diversity', which is another watchword for the Sixth Root Race. If you can hold and experience the diversity of different DNA frequencies in the various species of animal and plant, and if you can hold the frequency signatures encoded in the DNA and the phenotypic[7] physical vehicles, then you will see that all life is interconnected. This is not so much a case of seeing it, but rather of feeling it, at a very profound level. This interconnection is the reason why there is so much homology[8] or similarity of DNA structure, between the different species of animal and plant. It is also why you will be able to access these different frequencies, for they are buried very deeply within you, within what may be described as your 'genetic psyche'.

To feel the frequency vibrations of a worm, a turtle, a bull, a swan, will give you a very different perspective on life, and as you let the walls of fear drop, and the gates of Eternity slowly open, you will feel, ever more deeply, the profundity of the Divine connection that runs throughout life. It vibrates and resonates in light, and finds its physical form in the vibrational structures that are represented in your genetic make-up, not just on the physical level, but also on the etheric level. Some of you recognise this intuitively, and are seeking expression of this profound realisation. Again, just invoke the light, and the light will help you to access the information that you need in this grand adventure.

The new breed of frequency-holders, whom some have termed the 'living librarians'[9] of the planetary frequencies, are older souls who were present when the First Root Race was seeded into the Planet. They were here at the start. They have varied backgrounds, drawn from the different backdrops of specialist frequencies that were originally involved in building the Planet. They include members of the Lion people[10] otherwise known as the Paschats, the Dragon tribes[11], the Reptilian[12] and Pleiadian[13] frequencies, the Sirian White Lodge[14], an assortment or collective grouping of Amphibian[15] frequencies, and strong representation from the Insect[16] collective societies. Though some of you may find this a little more difficult, there are members who have worked in conjunction with the Spider[17] frequencies. These have a particularly strong lineage in working with specific heart frequencies through sound and vibration.

DNA as a Frequency-Holder

All of the above frequencies, as well as many not mentioned here, were present at the inception of the First Root Race and have continued to incarnate in human physical form at various times. Their job, as frequency-holders, is to hold the new alignment of DNA vibrations that are both heralded and transformed through the Photon Belt, and by the various other mechanisms that have already been mentioned. The ancient wisdom that will be cultivated by an alignment of these frequencies and their retention within the etheric DNA structure of the human race, will help seed into humanity a new perception of frequency-holding and vibrations.

Why is it that some people are drawn to some animals rather than to others? Why is it that people's affinity with animals is often greater than with other human beings? Part of the reason has to do with each individual's ancestral lineage[18] and family focus[19]. The family of frequencies represented (albeit incompletely) above gives a clue to the pattern of this new vibration and alignment. In the new pattern, a frequency-holder or 'librarian' will shuttle through the different DNA frequencies endemic to the Planet. As these frequencies become reactivated by the Photon Belt, their etheric and astral counterparts will, in turn, reactivate some of the older mental alignments[20] seeded in the mental planes. Through further invocation of the

Paramatman Light, these older frequencies can then be re-anchored into matter. In this way, many old, dormant frequencies can be re-activated and brought into physical substance in a way that has not been possible for some considerable time.

The Sixth Root Race Symphony

The situation is somewhat akin to that of a great symphony, say by Beethoven or Mozart, in which particular themes are played out and reprised within each movement. For our purposes, each movement represents a specific Root Race, and each has an unlimited potentiality of themes. Part of the operation of bringing together the Sixth Root Race frequencies will be to combine alignments (i.e. 'themes') from the older Root Race frequencies and this will be done in a combination that represents the *'créme de la créme'* of these frequencies. This will be particularly intriguing for many of you.

You will find, at various points in your life, that your energy system will become activated like a light-house. A strong, clear signal of intent, frequency intent, will be broadcast by you as a tuning-in or recognition signal. This will have been initiated by the upgrading of your DNA signal, and will in turn, resonate with, and activate, the DNA signals in others around you. As this frequency modality spreads around the family of light workers, and is seeded and earthed into the Planet, then others around will be able to pick it up and bring it into their own internal space for processing and earthing.

Light-Houses of Frequency Intent

The information contained within each of these 'light-houses' will be seeded into specific people, or picked up by specific groups of people, according to their vibration. The timing and mode of switching these 'light-houses' on will be critical. It is similar to the switching on and off of genes[21] in the developmental process, or in the development of new life, whether it be human, mammalian, amphibian, or other.

As these new frequencies are switched on by sympathetic resonance in each of you, there will be a tidal swell of indifference from many people around you. You will be connecting at a deeper level within your being than ever before, yet it will seem at first as if this is occurring in a vacuum. Do not be deceived by this. The indifference will change, and it is worth appreciating the reasons for it: it is just that those around you do not yet have the correct equipment or alignment within their karmic cordings[22] to receive the new transmissions. This is extremely important to remember, in order that the initial sense of loss, and the subsequent feeling of coming home, that will accompany these new frequency bursts, should not be invalidated by those around you. Feel only the frequencies.

So, in this re-awakening of the new frequencies, when the Sixth Root Race thought form, as the grand conductor of the human and extra-terrestrial orchestra, raises the baton of Divine Intent, then will the new music, the new frequencies, come crashing through into your consciousness. The extent and power of this new movement, of this reprise of the old Root Races, combined with the new dawn of the Sixth Root Race melody and rhythm, will provide a bedrock of intent for your continued invocation of the new frequencies. Invoke these new light-houses of information, these new beacons of frequency-rapport between yourself and others. The light-houses will not be limited to those in human form. They will influence and affect other forms of life, both terrestrial and extra-terrestrial. This is the Way and the Truth.

In this context, the very apt term 'light-house' refers to a light worker. A light-house emits periodic bursts of energy, which bathe the landscape or seascape, and indicate the way home to the shore. This serves as an illustration of the function of these metaphorical 'light-houses': the frequency-bursts that they emit help to light the way home into your heart, into the Divine Ocean of Love.

Connecting with Future Aspects of Ourselves

Speaking of the Sixth Root Race in this way is paradoxical. On the one hand you are invoking a new thought form and manifesting it into physicality, and yet in another sense this has already happened, because the time lines that you travel are an illusion. Many of your authors have written about time travel, and how, if you go back into the past, then you can modify it and consequently change the future. Some of your television programmes, like *Sliders*, talk of this concept. What is certainly true today, is that future aspects of yourself are returning to the present to connect with you, and to ensure that the path and time line that you tread will become evident, and will be followed according to Divine Intent. I hear you ask, then: what about free will, free choice? Free will and choice operate on different levels within this scenario. First, you have the choice to ignore your future aspect, and to remain segregated if you so wish. Second, your future aspect has shown free will by coming back in time to connect with you more assuredly in the present. All of this is possible because the twin karmic points of death and time enable this transition and connection to occur[23].

Your connection with your future selves will be subtle at first, although it does form an interesting aspect to Sixth Root Race reality. As time dissolves, and you become multidimensional, it is true that you can be in many different places and times at once. This is exciting, but it will require some adjustment of your psyche, which may be overwhelmed at first by all the different sense impressions coming in. This is natural and to be expected, and you should not be concerned by it.

Multi-dimensional reality will be another key aspect in Sixth Root Race living.

The light that will illuminate the path of multi-dimensional reality will be intense, like a beacon. It is not something to be treated frivolously: it will require patience, dedication, trust, and above all, courage — courage to let go of the older perspectives and limitations of life in the Fifth Root Race. As the light begins to flow into your heart, you will come to sense a new connection within yourself. The light is everywhere, and if you can connect with it ever more deeply, and become one with it, then you, too, can be everywhere. This is, in one sense, an aspect of God-realisation, but the profundity of this statement, and the depth of connection required to realise this aspect, are extreme. God-realisation is something that you all aspire to, but which the vast majority have yet to achieve.

The Paramatman Light Through the Ages

The Sixth Root Race is anchored in light, and more specifically in the Paramatman Light. This is the Divine Experiment. For many of you, who have not connected with the Paramatman Light in this incarnation, it may be useful to connect back with your older Egyptian days, where the Paramatman Light was deeply revered and honoured within the Early and Middle Egyptian dynasties. By the later years in Egypt, the true heart connection with the Paramatman had been lost, and replaced by a more dispersed and diverse aspect of consciousness. Our mission today is to reinstate the purity of that connection with the Paramatman that was present in ancient Egyptian times, but at the same time to raise it to a new octave of brilliance. Much of the imagery and culture of those times is for many encompassed by the face depicted in Tutankhamun's golden funeral mask. There is a clue in this, as well as in the many statues made in earlier Egyptian times. If you invoke your intuition and older memories, it should become clearer to you what the importance of this imagery is, and how it is linked to the Paramatman.

The Paramatman is everywhere, was everywhere, and will be everywhere. So just as the 'light-houses' of the present are opening up to the new frequencies demanded by the new age, so it is that you can also recover some of these older frequencies, and their significance from the older Root Races.

The same is true of the Atlantean age. The Paramatman Light had a different presentation then, being more consolidated within the various temple settings that were such an important part of that culture. The different animal life representations and extra-terrestrial frequencies helped to bring through the force of the Paramatman Light, but the events surrounding the realignment or removal of the more exquisite Divine Frequencies led to a dissolution of the Paramatman within the physical realms at that time. The frequencies were there for everyone to invoke and connect with, but instead of embracing the Paramatman in their hearts, the inhabitants decided to realign their energy systems with the lower chakras, thereby shattering the unity and diversity of mind and body then demanded by the Paramatman.

What is happening today is a re-run of the changes that occurred then, but a re-run with a difference. The invocation of the Paramatman has been made, the call has been heard from on High, and the light that is now streaming down into the Planet is being anchored within the minds and *hearts* of men and women, rather than in the other centres. This is a critical difference from the Atlantean times, and it will be the saving grace for humanity, although not in a conventional sense. What it means is that the grace and beauty of the Divine Plan can be resurrected by the intent that we invoke within our hearts and minds, through a true alignment of both.

The Crystalline Matrix Energies

> Before the Atlantean times, in the Lemurian period, the presence of the Paramatman was clearly understood and held within the hearts of men and women. The serenity and beauty of that connection can also be accessed today as part of the recapitulation of the Root Races. That Lemurian purity, coupled with the Atlantean power of Intent and the Egyptian crystalline matrix of Will, or Intent, can all be harmonised in a new and vibrant format. 'Crystalline matrix' may seem a rather strange way of referring to some of the more ancient aspects of the Egyptian civilisation, but the fact is that within the various temple settings in that culture, very high-frequency crystalline energies were invoked. These followed on from some of the Atlantean crystalline practices, but they became more segregated and focused in Egyptian times through the sacred geometry that was used to harmonise and resonate with them. This crystalline matrix is again being invoked in the Sixth Root Race.

What is meant by crystalline matrix of Intent? In the first place, many of us have our origins within the crystalline and gaseous frequencies as we started our journey of ascent into matter from the Divine Ocean. As we moved through numerous crystalline phases, we built up a resonant crystalline frequency-structure or harmonic that remains deeply buried within us today. In the past this ancient aspect of ourselves was recognised, and enhanced through various energy practices performed in temples. The sacred geometry, the alignment of size and space to cosmic and galactic dimensions, was but a part of this. Just as each crystal has a perfect internal geometry that is a representation of its essence, the same is true of our own crystalline frequencies: we each have our own sacred geometry. In Egyptian times this was realised, and pulled into the physical by the construction of various buildings and temples which helped to amplify, and resonated within, these inherent frequencies. The Pyramids are but one such example, and the difference in their sizes was a way in which the different crystalline qualities could be enhanced and brought out into the open.

The other means of amplification was through a deeper connection with our star-brothers and sisters. Those extra-terrestrials who resonate on a higher crystalline frequency were able, once a harmonic resonance had been established, to come into the physical and subtler space of some of the trance channels[24] of those times. They connected directly, and merged within that physical space. The crystalline frequency that was then set up by this merging established a portal, or dimensional doorway, between us and our star-brothers and sisters. The sacred geometry of the time helped to invoke this connection through the purity of mathematical calculation, and so it was that one could focus with a crystalline object such as amethyst or quartz, intuit the special geometry of that crystal, and use it as an amplification device to connect with the higher crystalline frequencies. The Egyptians, and the Atlanteans before them, were extremely interested in the experimentation that developed through these special and sacred connections.

Crystalline Geometry and Sacred Divination

The Crystal Skulls represented, in a special way, the sum total of all these crystalline frequencies and they facilitated the development of crystalline geometry and sacred divination. There is the possibility for much of this to return through the Sixth Root Race vibration, and to build on the octave that was developed in the past.

The same is true of sound. There was, in ancient Atlantean times, a group of people known as crystal singers. The closest analogy today is with opera singers who are able to reach the peaks of a purity of note and resonance that is second to none. In the past, these crystalline frequencies were also allied to the sound *form*, which is the wave of energy that is directed by sound. Through an alignment of sound and a specific crystalline frequency, it became possible to build up a resonant harmonic that could open up dimensional doorways in space and time. This practice was less well-known in ancient Egypt, but had been developed to quite a high degree during Atlantean times.

It should become clear that the crystalline matrix of energy that was initially seeded by the Crystal Skulls, also set up a deep resonance or memory during our own early stages of evolution, as we ascended through the gaseous and crystalline phases. This was then expressed through sacred and divine geometry, so that the different crystalline nature of each of us could be amplified and merged in a variety of ways. These techniques included crystal healing, crystal singing, and crystal dowsing of new doorways and dimensional access points. The latter particularly was accomplished through the help of our extra-terrestrial friends. All of this reflects the light path that was taken at that time.

Of course, in the balance of Divine Intent, there is always the question of the dark path, and this too was pursued, by using crystals that were seeded with dark intent. It was perhaps inevitable that there would be a clash, a collision, between these two paths. For many of us who practised both light and dark crystalline magic in those ancient days, there is much internal and external repair-work to be done on our systems. This must be completed before we can truly access the purest and most divine of vibrations that can be made manifest through the crystalline energy.

Following on from this, one expression or intent of the Sixth Root Race is to connect more deeply with the Divine Fire and the Divine Light that are present within our true crystalline nature. This is what really matters, and it is through the various sacred crystalline practices of old that we shall be able to reconnect with these ancient skills, these expressions of our divinity. This is the beauty of what will be made manifest, and just as in the past, our old extra-terrestrial brothers and sisters will be involved in this Divine experiment, and will share their knowledge and love in the process. These are indeed exciting times.

These crystalline energies have a very important role to play in the formation of the Sixth Root Race. The purity of intent and invocation of these frequencies will be vitally important, and caution will be needed: caution that you have the physical, and subtler, purity of intent to hold these new, powerful energies as they become manifest, and enter your space. This type of work is not something that can be entered into in an unprepared manner. A great deal of preparation and consolidation of your energy systems is needed before the true vibrations can be invoked and held within your physical spaces. **Preparation** is the key word, and the greater the preparation, then the better the results, and the deeper the connection.

It is now time to move on from this discussion of the Sixth Root Race crystalline energies, and to consider the importance of the Dolphin Frequency on the Planet today.

Dolphin Energies

It is perhaps ironic that you have had, right under your noses, an expressed energy frequency of Intent that has great purity and joy, as embodied in the dolphin. You are beginning to realise this, as may be seen through the various ways in which dolphins communicate, and help to heal the sick and disabled. Dolphins also have telepathic consciousness, and so represent, in a sense, the frequency-rapport of the Sixth Root Race. You have yet fully to appreciate the magnitude of the work that has been undertaken by the dolphins on Earth's behalf.

Since the Atlantean times, and more recently in particular, the dolphins have represented the frequency guardians of the Planet, the frequency holders of the renegade DNA that remained dormant within your space. This has been very necessary, as mankind has needed time to heal the wounds, on all levels, that were a direct result of the Atlantean cataclysm. Symbolically, as Atlantis sank into the sea, so did the responsibility for guardianship of the Planet. The dolphins have their roots within the extra-terrestrial frequencies encompassed by the Sirian White Lodge energies, and to a limited extent before that in other planetary systems such as Alcyone[25]. They have acted as Earth's guardians for many centuries, and this task, which has continued unnoticed, has been of key significance.

The time has now come for this responsibility to be passed back to the human race so that the dolphins can move forward as part of their own evolutionary progression, and seed their specific frequencies within other dimensions and forms. The debt owed to them by the Planet is indeed immense. This may seem difficult to conceptualise, or even to fathom at first, but a simple exercise may help you to establish a connection. When you have a moment of peace and tranquillity, it may be helpful to imagine your physical body-shape transforming into that of a dolphin. You will find if you do this that you take on the characteristics or qualities or feelings embodied by the dolphin energy; including their sense of lightness of spirit, their fun, and the collective nature of their consciousness. These are but a few aspects of their being and you may connect with an array of other dolphin vibrations. Experiencing some of these dolphin frequencies may help you to understand the unique role played by the them.

The Dolphin Collective

The higher aspect of the dolphin vibration forms what is known as the Dolphin Collective. This is a very tightly-bound unit, and can be accessed across vast distances in time and space. It has a central core of intent that resonates with the Spiritual Hierarchy and on the higher astral and mental planes, and it is therefore able to connect with the higher Divinity of the Planet, and the Planetary frequency holders: the intuitive connection of the minds and hearts of the dolphin community has links with the Highest of the High. The collective intent of the dolphin is extremely pure, crystalline, and light. The sense of fun and enjoyment expressed by dolphins at being in the physical is a particularly beautiful aspect of their consciousness. You would do well to emulate some of these features.

The dolphins, as guardians and frequency holders for the Planet and its living species, have held the fabric of etheric and mental light together in a particular and profound way. By harnessing their highest collective signature note, they have succeeded in aligning and harmonising many of the more discordant DNA vibrations that have been seeded, uninvited, into the Planet over many generations. This has been a particularly difficult piece of work, and has required a sacrifice of significant proportions within the Dolphin Collective. All of this has gone on unseen and unknown by humankind, and it will remain so for some time to come. By clearing the astral and etheric vibrations of ill-intent within a number of specific frequency ranges and harmonics, the dolphin collective has played a critical part in the establishment of the Sixth Root Race frequency. By harmonising and broadcasting a specific DNA love vibration through the etheric, the dolphins, as a collective, have prepared much of the ground needed for the transformation that is to come.

The call has gone out from the Dolphin Collective to many people to seek ways to harmonise and merge with it. The merging that is to come will set in motion the process of specific transference of their keynote frequencies into the collective wave experienced within humanity today. This is no easy task, and it will require dedication and commitment by a number of light workers. However, the rewards and the beauty of this process will make it most worthwhile.

Connecting with Dolphin Frequencies

Apart from anchoring the light within their different centres, the dolphins have also cleared out significant chunks of slower-frequency energy from the oceanic depths. Much of this has been linked to the older Atlantean frequencies, and has been a necessary precursor to many of the shifts arising within your consciousness. As forerunners for mankind in this epoch, the dolphins have anchored the light and love from the Divine Heights into the Planet on a collective basis. As the Sixth Root Race now emerges within humanity, it is the turn of humankind to take over this role again in earnest, and the collective pulse established by the dolphins will then be anchored in the human form more specifically. This is an important reason for you now to connect sincerely and deeply with the dolphin energies. The transference of the frequencies and information held within the Dolphin Collective must be passed over to you by around 2020, so that the next stepping-stone in the emergence of the Sixth Root Race can be reached.

Dolphins as Frequency-Holders

The dolphin frequency has its roots in Atlantean times. There arose a paramount need for a species other than humankind to anchor the vibrations of light and love to the Planet: since those times this task has been selflessly performed by the dolphins. The vibrational signature that has been emitted by the dolphins has, as its source, a holographic rapport[26] with the Paramatman Light. This means that while there is a direct connection with the Paramatman Light, there is also a resonance that was established as a holograph which continued to connect with the dolphin frequencies when the direct connection with the Paramatman was not always present. This allowed a continuity of connection between the Paramatman and the dolphins at all times.

An interesting question in all of this is how the dolphins have acted as library-holders of the planetary frequency. Firstly, they have a flexible DNA structure and blue-print that enabled the mental vibrations within their collective to be held and dispersed throughout the Planet in a deep and powerful manner. They have been assisted by a number of different species in this process, including whales. Secondly, their DNA frequencies have held deep transformative energies and vibrations. The anchoring of the light within their physical units has also meant that their DNA frequencies have contained a collective pulse or spark, which has resonated with many different vertebrate species, including mammals and fish. In the Sixth Root Race this process needs to be expanded on by humankind to incorporate many invertebrate species such as spiders, insects, sponges, and many others. The light will then help to raise the harmonic frequency of the Planet in its totality, for in truth, the changes demanded by the new vibrations require the raising of the frequency of all living forms on Earth. Just as you take the pulse beat of your heart from the Planet, so do all other living forms, and they too have to accommodate this change within their physical, etheric, and astral aspects.

The dolphin collective has set the scene, and over the next twenty to thirty years it will be passing to you the baton of responsibility in this Divine evolutionary process. It is, therefore, essential that as many light workers as possible begin to connect with the dolphin collective, which, as has been demonstrated, is an essential component of the formation of the Sixth Root Race.

Chapter 4 • New Frequencies

The vast array of new frequencies that will be bombarding both the Planet and our internal and external spaces, will require, on our part, great flexibility, stability, and resourcefulness if we are to house them within our space. Like old-fashioned radio sets that can only receive within a limited band-width, we are at present limited in our ability to receive these signals. In reality there is a multitude of stations waiting to be tuned into, each with its brand of information, music, and humour. The challenge that is presented to many light workers today is to increase their flexibility, and their capacity to receive and earth[1] these new frequency-signatures.

One critical aspect of this process is the recognition that it is important to cultivate a very broad band-width. Although specialisation within certain frequency types will be necessary and desirable, really it is the breadth and flexibility that are crucial. An ability to trawl the depths of the slower frequencies, and to offer these up to the light, needs to be balanced with a capacity to soar to the highest new frequencies, and to hold them within our space. This is no easy task: it requires a chameleon-like capacity and flexibility of our system.

Preparation Through Clearing

Building a broad band-width requires several factors. Firstly, there needs to be an ongoing programme of clearing one's internal and external space of any slower vibrations that have remained rooted within one from the past. For many people, this is synonymous with the solar plexus centre, but in fact it also encompasses all the other chakra centres. Secondly, any defects in the etheric body[2] need to be repaired, and this should be accompanied by the adoption of procedures for continually cleansing and regenerating the aura. This latter point is especially difficult, given the amount of static[3] generated by electromagnetic sources that are present around us all the time. Such sources include cars, computers, televisions, radios, aeroplanes, and so forth. It is therefore essential to bathe the aura continuously in light and to ground[4] our physical space with Earth energies. In the subtler planes, a dedication to, and concentration on, clearing karmic associations with others, and working with our guides in a group setting, are equally important. Integral to this is finding a way in which to bring the signal[5] down into our physical bodies from the higher mental and the higher astral planes.

This overall process of clearing can be likened to a concertina of subtle bodies, many hundreds of them, some of which are in alignment with each other and some of which are not. If any body is out of alignment with another, then it prevents a clear signal from being passed down the line, and the more bodies that are out of alignment the harder it becomes for *any* signal to pass down the line. Another way of looking at this is in terms of recapturing the fragmentation of our subtle bodies that has arisen over many lifetimes. Each life can be represented by one of these subtle bodies, and as we pass through more and more lives, we develop a greater degree of fragmentation. Eventually, however, we need to bring these fragments back together, and this can only be done through a driven process of collection within the astral and mental planes. This is obviously an extremely lengthy process, which takes place over many lifetimes, and involves clearing out the karmic 'wash' from many, many past lives.

Guides, and the Ascending New Frequencies

As if all of this was not enough, we also need to cultivate a flexibility and a frequency-rapport with our guides whereby recognition and communication are instantaneous.

> Each of you will have a guide who acts as a central doorkeeper[6], and it will be essential to connect very deeply with this being. The central doorkeeper oversees the different frequencies that you are able to connect with as you progress up and down the inner planes. The concentrated pattern of recognition of your inner guidance[7], combined with a strict cleansing process, will enable

you to anchor the light more effectively within your body.

The next step is to practise connecting with the different frequencies. Preferably this should be done in a group setting, since the voltage generated will be much greater than on an individual basis. It will also allow a greater sea of frequencies to be accessed by the collective imprint of karmic connections[8]. This is most important.

During this process of connection with new frequencies, do not be surprised if you encounter things that you cannot afterwards express in words. At the time of connection they may seem quite straightforward, but often much — if not all — recollection of the experience will subsequently be lost from your conscious mind. This is to be expected, since it is part of the process of ascending within your internal space to the higher planes, and then receiving the information: although when you come back into the physical the conscious imprint is lost, the information is stored within your system at another level for future access and activation. The demands placed upon your physical vehicles in this process will be significant, in particular the stresses on your nervous and emotional systems.

A sense of emotional isolation can arise after deeper connections within. It is best to attach no importance to this, since it is a by-product of the ascendancy into new frequency-vibrations and of the process of anchoring them into the Planet. Too many light workers become totally 'burnt-out' and are, to coin a phrase, "no earthly good" to anyone. So plenty of rest and relaxation are essential.

This is a somewhat brief introduction to some of the key aspects of connecting with the new frequencies. Each person and each group will forge an identifying signal and feature that will be built upon, and used, by the Spiritual Hierarchy in accordance with the Divine Plan. It is this form of selfless service which will also mark a cornerstone in the Sixth Root Race emergence. The number of light workers receiving the wake-up call is increasing, and they are being drawn through the karmic ties of love to connect more deeply with themselves and their loved-ones. As this process builds, the call for selfless service, born of love for the Divine, will spread like wild-fire around the Planet once a series of collective frequency signatures has been achieved. This point is still some years away, since many light workers still need to awaken from their deep slumbers, and realise who they are, and what their Divine mission is.

New Frequencies and Dimensional Doorways

The symphony of frequencies that are being, and will be, seeded into the Planet is sublime. Several dimensional doorways have been constructed on the inner planes over the last few years, doorways which will provide an access point into the Planet for some of them. The extra-terrestrial doorway that was opened in April 1997 is one example, as is a second doorway that opened in September 1997, as part of the initiation of the 'Mind of One' programme. Several smaller doorways have also been opened.

All of these doorways are anchored within the higher mental planes and, therefore, provide access points into the Planet for very specific frequencies of Intent. This is part of the segregation that was mentioned earlier. The quality of light and love, from both your star-brothers and sisters and the Divine Hierarchy of Spiritual Beings who today are gracing Earth physically and on the inner planes, is second to none. It will serve to increase the harmonic vibration of the Planet in conjunction with its increasing planetary heart-beat. The two complement one another, and the challenge for all physical beings enmeshed, within this web of change, is to harmonise with both frequency accords, from within and without. In practice, this means that you are all currently experiencing an extremely acute point of pressure within your internal and external spaces.

The other effect of anchoring these doorways within the higher mental planes is that each light worker, through perseverance, love, and dedication, must earn the right to access them. This is not meant in a critical way: the experiences that are thrown up for each of you, as you beat a path to the higher mental planes and the doorways, will provide an immeasurable tidal swell of experience and endurance. This will enable you to anchor the new frequencies in a much more effortless way. The search for doorways will provide the training ground for strengthening your physical and other systems so that once you have connected with the doorways, you will then be able, by virtue of the work you have put in, to hold and handle the new frequencies. Instead of being burnt-out by the quality of the light and love that are being emitted, you will be strong enough to handle it.

The Doorway of the Mind of One

These new dimensional access points are highly significant, and it is worth going into more detail on each of them. Firstly, to further what has been said before, the Mind of One is a term that refers to the Divine Invocation of the new dawn, and the new frequencies that are demanded of the Sixth Root Race and the Aquarian age, as initiated by Sai Baba[9]. Secondly, the term refers to the collective consciousness of all light workers on the Planet at this time, and to the collective intent to harmonise all their frequencies with the Divine Intent. The Mind of One, therefore, refers to the Divine Fire of the Divine Father, and to the transformation of frequencies that will sweep through the Planet. It represents, in a fundamental way, a stripping away of the old, and the instigation of the new, through the invocation and drawing-down of the Collective Intent of the Divine Father, Meher Baba[10].

Accessing the quality of light and love within the doorway of the Mind of One is a precise and specific role for all light workers. Merging ever more deeply with this vibration, and pulling it into physical matter, is essential. Once anchored within the Planet, the new light-frequencies can be used in very specific ways. For example, they can be directed at all that provides offence in relation to slower-frequency activities. This light and love represent the sword of Truth, Fire, and Divinity which can cut through the miasmas of old occult practices; old survivalistic and selfish activities involving the use of physical and emotional suffering to control others, whether they be of human, animal, or plant form, can be targeted, transformed, and banished. This is a key which needs to be invoked with all our heart and with all our love, for there is much work to be done in clearing all practices which defile the purity of our own divinity and love. Feel into your heart, and you will know intuitively which of those activities is offensive to you, and which need to be removed, transformed, and taken up into the light.

The Extra-Terrestrial Doorway

The second doorway is an extra-terrestrial access point, and it has a rather different focus, being currently used specifically to usher new extra-terrestrial frequencies into the Planet for a defined period of time. Much of the preparatory work has already been done, and this doorway was activated throughout the latter part of 1999 and during 2000. Again, accessing the new frequencies will require an openness of mind, a suspension of normal perception, if the vibrations are to take form and substance. The possibilities for new forms of communication will provide unique channelling opportunities for many light workers and the opportunity to connect with old friends. It is certainly something of an understatement to say that there is high excitement on the inner planes at this prospect.

The Third ('Unspoken') Doorway

These two doorways will be supplemented, at a later date, by a third, more substantial one. This will not occur for some years, and it will only be activated once a significant proportion of light workers have attained their optimum operating frequency, and when many of the slower-frequency energies of the Planet have been offered up to the light. The majesty of this future opening will, as with the previous doorways, defy description, and furthermore this third doorway will be a direct link with the Divine Father Himself, Meher Baba. It will also initiate a brand new octave of Divinity within the Planet, and will be linked to what has been termed the 'Unspoken Word'[11] of Meher Baba. The magnitude and majesty of this will be totally beyond words, beyond anything that your imagination can conceive at this time.

For those not acquainted with Meher Baba's Unspoken Word, some background is necessary. During his life Meher Baba spent over forty years in total silence, communicating by hand signals and an alphabet board for much of this time. Although He dropped his body in 1969, He had always said that He would break His silence with the release of the Unspoken Word. The release of the Unspoken Word will represent the clarion call for the new millennium and the new age, as demanded by the Sixth Root Race. There has been much speculation as to the timing and form of release of the Unspoken Word by Meher Baba. However this may be, we shall know it when it comes.

So, as you can see, some aspects of the Divine Plan are beginning to take shape. All of this is really an outline sketch. The detail will, as in all things Divine, be filled in as and when appropriate, according to perfect timing and circumstances.

The energies will continue to push higher and higher as the new frequency rapports rain down into the Planet. Just as we connect with our highest guides, and invoke the higher vibrations, so the Planetary vibration that is being driven upwards by the Photon Belt, will assist in this invocation. The process will work through, and in harmony with, a deep rapport with the energies that are building at this time. Such is the beauty of the Divine Plan.

Connect ever more deeply with your own divine truth, and the Divine Will. Invoke the light; feel the light, and love the light as your own. Feel its intensity, and link with it at all times.

Tidal Waves of Energy

As you connect with the new frequencies, it will become clear as you go along, that the energy matrix is not dissimilar to a tidal wave of energy. The in-breath and out-breath of the Prime Creator[12] established an original matrix of energy-flow akin to the ebb and flow of the oceans. This tidal flow of energy is drawn down through the various planes until it is manifested in the physical realms through the intake and out-flow of pranic[13] energy. This pranic flow is part of your original connection with the Creator; another aspect is that in the current dynamic inter-play of energies, various secondary factors are involved, such as planetary energies, the Photon Belt, and the input of light waves from the Divine and the Spiritual Hierarchy Itself. What is different is that authority has been granted to increase the power and input of these energies as they are stepped down into the Planet. As in all energy movements, there are times when there is a build-up of energy, a damming effect as some of the slower and denser frequencies are pulled apart and lifted into the light. Sometimes the density of these frequencies is such that the tidal effect is amplified and pooled, and then the tides can become really extremely broad and powerful. This is, in a way, what is happening on Earth. The ebb and flow of light vibrations is being stepped up, and as it encounters 'resistance' (and we use this term advisedly), then the tidal swell increases until the slower-frequency energy has been released.

In the current karmic play on your Planet, there are, and

will continue to be, many such tidal swells at work. This, as has been mentioned before, is particularly acute on the astral planes, and to a lesser degree on the mental planes. This tidal interplay needs to be registered by all light workers, since it will greatly influence their effectiveness; their capacity to bring down and anchor the light. By analogy, there is little point in attempting various difficult outdoor tasks during a storm. So it is on the inner planes: when these 'astral storms' are active, it is important to find that point of balance where nothing can harm or influence you. Instead of being battered around by the astral 'wind', you need to be firmly rooted within your consciousness and your own space, which is neither light nor dark, but just a deep resting-point, away from the interplay of frequencies. You will know when stormy periods are upon you, not only in terms of the external manifestation of energies, but in terms of your own waking and resting energy levels. When you feel deeply tired, then is the time to rest — there is little point in over-straining the system. This is often one of the harder lessons for light workers to learn but in the long run it is worth heeding.

There will come a point in the years ahead when this tidal interplay will begin to subside, and the new energies will be firmly anchored within your Planet. The task that all light workers are presented with is to remain grounded during these turbulent times, while emitting the light-frequency signal that is your signature.

Clearing Astral Waste

As with all tidal waves, there will be large quantities of debris, or in this case, slow, dense frequencies, literally hanging around. The 'cosmic clean-up' operation that will be required will be substantial — it has, in fact, already commenced, but there remain major areas of stagnation and difficulty. Old radio-active waste areas, old plague grounds, old burial sites, old battlefields, and killing fields, and other areas of stagnant negative energy all need to be cleared. In this respect, we are not primarily referring to the physical, three-dimensional sense in which all the rubbish and pollution need (as indeed they do) to be cleared up: all these stagnant energies have their astral counterparts, and it is these which now require urgent attention.

The role of many light workers will be as 'drain cleaners' or 'waste specialists'. The clearing of the astral garbage is a huge task, and one that will take many years to complete; and as the new frequencies and energies enter the Earth, the urgent necessity for this work will become overpowering. For many, the first reaction to the idea of 'cleaning the drains' is, understandably, to run in the opposite direction. However, the Divine works in mysterious ways, and since you are seeking the light and beauty of your Planet, this undertaking of 'slime-control' or 'astral waste-cleaning' services may be pivotal to your development.

It is fair to say that we never get something for nothing. As indicated earlier, our ability to connect with and span the widest breadth of frequencies is essential, but being able to work with the slowest frequencies, to clear and send them to the light, is equally important. When working with the slower frequencies, there will always be a reciprocity in our ability to connect with the light, and to access the higher ones. It is rather like *earning* the right to connect with all of them. Just as in everyday life we all have tasks to perform in order to earn our livelihood, and are thus able to enjoy the contrasts — the periods of relaxation, and the pursuit of pleasurable activities, so it is on the inner planes: the act of clearing and cleansing astral waste allows all light workers to earn the right to access at all times the higher frequencies and the more vibrant energies.

You will also come to realise that there are those amongst us who will have specialist jobs in this work. Some will specialise in particular aspects of slow-frequency energy salvage, while others will focus on directing and processing these different frequencies towards the light. Know that this is all perfectly orchestrated, and that those tasks and specialist roles that you undertake are perfectly suited for your energy systems in this incarnation.

So when you wake up in the morning feeling tired, and uncertain about whether you really did have a good night's sleep, it may well be linked to the work that you do on the inner planes. Universal work of this nature is always twenty-four hours a day.

Astral Doorways

We have spoken a little of the dimensional doorways that are opening into your Planet from the higher mental planes. There are, of course, astral doorways which are also opening. Some care needs to be taken in connecting with these, since they will bring through a much more forceful imprint of light and dark energies, which can be overwhelming. It is, therefore, advisable to work with those doorways that can be utilised to invoke the light. This is not to say that darker doorways will not actually open up in your space from time to time — the timing of such openings is often dependent upon planetary and solar system conditions. These darker doorways will tend to be activated at night, and will be access points for slower-frequency energies to enter your space. It is fairly easy to recognise some of these openings by the reaction of your body. If, for no reason, you become fearful, anxious, feeling a lot of activation around your solar plexus area, then it is highly likely that slower-frequency energies are entering your space. Some people have experienced more extreme examples, such as feeling pinned down to their beds and unable to move because of some unseen force. Although these experiences may be confused with the state in which, prior to sleep, your mind remains alert but your muscles go to sleep[14], there still remain a number of cases where slow-frequency energies take on a much more physical quality.

The best way of dealing with these situations is to call in the 'group', and to operate on a collective basis by invoking higher-frequency energies into your space. This should raise your frequency-vibration, and enable you to avoid being caught up in the slower-frequency vibrations of fear, distrust, anger, hatred, and so on[15]. This is important to note, because with so much loose, slow-frequency energy flying around in the astral planes, it is almost inevitable that from time to time you will be affected by these doorways opening and closing. The darker doorways tend to be activated in a cyclical fashion, and if your experiences are recurrent, it may be as well to note the timing of these events, so that you can plan ahead, and not be in a vulnerable position at such times — the slower-frequency energies will always target you when you are at your most vulnerable.

Because of these slower-frequency doorways, there remains the desire and need to bring the light doorways into your internal space. The two doorways (the Mind of One and Extra-Terrestrial) that have been mentioned are excellent starting points and since everything on the inner planes is but a thought away, you need do no more than to invoke the connection to them. By doing so, you will be sending out a call and a thought form that will, with practice on your part, build a bridge to the doorway. This requires, as in many things esoteric, great persistence and dedication if you are not used to this way of working. However, invoking a connection with these doorways, according to Highest or Greatest Good, will ultimately ensure that you get a response, and that you set out on the path to a deeper connection with them.

Working with the Doorway of the Mind of One

The Doorway of the Mind of One represents the sum total, at this time, of what the frequency vibrations of the Sixth Root Race will contain. As the Divine Father Meher Baba has proclaimed the advent of the Sixth Root Race, so the associated frequencies are unfolding, and are stepped-down from the mental, through the astral to the physical planes. Linking with this particular doorway carries with it a responsibility to act and invoke according to the higher principles of love and light. Invocation of these energies for purely selfish purposes and personal gain will represent a misuse, or even abuse, of them. This is why it is always important to prefix every invocation with the words "according to the Divine Plan" or "according to Greatest Good". This will ensure that in those circumstances where you are unsure as to the precise motivation of an invocation, then everything that follows is according to Universal and Divine Law. If what you invoke does not follow, then it may not have been according to highest good. Using these words is something of a safety mechanism or safety net. This is not to say that the energies cannot be invoked for self-healing. This is an appropriate use. But the manifestation of these Divine Frequencies for *collective* work, and the *collective* vibrational ascendancy is imperative.

It is perhaps a reflection on the human condition, and its ascendancy, that we now have access to such a doorway. The energies that are passing through it are of such great and exquisite beauty, that a small connection with them will feel as if a deep, Divine spark of love has been awakened within our various centres.

The invocation and guidance of Divine energies into areas of great slow frequency is what is required. This includes areas of great discord, areas where you may feel intuitively that there is an offence or imposition against a person's divinity, or in cases where there are real abuses of power, or activities of a much baser nature. The energies can be invoked to help clear old concentration camp sites, to halt the progressive march of child-abuse in our society, and also the misuse of animals. They can also help to engender a deeper sense of love and respect for our fellow human beings. These are all ways in which the Mind of One will be used to raise the frequency-vibration of the Planet.

So the commitment to become a part of the Mind of One, to invoke the love and the light of the Mind of One as a portal of Divine Energy, and to use this Divine Energy in a responsible and loving way, is of paramount importance. It is also extremely important for all light workers to invoke and access the Mind of One in a conscious and heart-felt way. This will help to raise the planetary frequency.

Reconnecting with our Extra-Terrestrial Heritage

The second doorway, the Extra-Terrestrial doorway, marks a reference point between the ascending frequency of Earth and its inhabitants, and the building of bridges with our star-brothers and sisters. There has been so much misunderstanding around the extra-terrestrial frequencies entering the Planet, so much sensationalising of extra-terrestrials, that it is sometimes difficult for people to have a balanced perspective on the matter. The fact that the human race exists should not be seen as a precondition for the lack of existence of life elsewhere. If anything, it should be taken as an indicator. What needs to be recognised is that just as we can access the Devic Kingdom[16] of the Planet with its vast array of frequencies and life-forms, so the same is true for frequencies which extend extra-terrestrially. This is a key point.

Extra-terrestrial frequencies can take on a range of different forms and energies. It is human preconception regarding their appearance that provides the main blockage to accessing these frequencies. However, over the next twenty years, the connection, and the construction of strong bridges of love and light with these new frequencies will become commonplace. This bridge-building will mark another essential aspect of the Sixth Root Race evolution, for if it becomes possible for us to become telepathic with our own friends and spiritual family here on Earth, then there is no reason why the same cannot happen with other life-forms, including extra-terrestrial life-forms. Our extra-terrestrial brothers and sisters have invested considerable time and effort in journeying to our inner space, and are keen that the emergence of the Sixth

Root Race manifesting on our Planet will be shared and understood within a much broader galactic perspective. The reason for this is simple. The frequencies being resurrected and constructed out of the older Root Races represent a recapitulation and re-awakening of humankind's true extra-terrestrial heritage. Just as the Sixth Root Race will become manifest on Earth, so equivalent transitions and developments can be inspired elsewhere in the galaxy.

In addition, our extra-terrestrial friends are keen to exchange frequencies on the Divine Path, and also to provide guidance, counsel, and above all, the shared experiences of true friendship and comradeship. That may sound odd to you, but since all creatures and all lifeforms are expressions of the Divine Plan, then it is an extraordinary opportunity for the different and diverse life-forms to share their experiences and to connect — at an incredibly deep level in some cases. This will require courage on the part of light workers. However, just as our extra-terrestrial friends have already travelled great distances to communicate with us, it now requires *our* collective will and love to bridge the gap, and to invite these new frequencies into our space. The opportunities are limitless.

> For most of you these old frequencies will represent a coming home within a deeper aspect of your soul's evolution. This is not meant in the sense of the final coming-home and union with God or the Divine, but that older aspects of yourself will be able to reconnect with you as never before. This experience will also provide an opportunity for future aspects, as mentioned earlier, to connect with you.

Releasing Old Extra-Terrestrial Thought Forms

> The thought forms around the extra-terrestrial doorway will build over the next fourteen years, and this groundwork will represent the template for allowing a re-balancing of some of the older extra-terrestrial frequencies. One of the reasons for the fear that many of you experience in relation to extra-

terrestrial frequencies goes back to the old Atlantean times, when the frequencies invoked were of a darker nature, and were, therefore, involved in the culmination and destruction of the Root Race of that age. There is a pressing need for you to clear this blockage or frequency-drain. As your body begins to remember some of your older extra-terrestrial encounters in human form, giving up and releasing these ancient experiences will become vitally important.

It should be recognised that there is a fundamental difference between the present day and the Atlantean times, when extra-terrestrial abominations abounded. The group and collective awareness of the Mind of One provides ample protection to all light workers from slower-frequency extra-terrestrials. As the release of old emotions associated with such beings takes place, so this shift in you will necessitate a karmic re-balancing for them. This will lead to a subsequent energy movement, and to release from their own bondage, their mental and phys-ical incarcerations. Thus, just as someone in a dispute between two people has to go forward and re-establish a dialogue and rebuild bridges, so it is that as the human race increases its fre-quency, the miasmas and thought forms associated with the older extra-terrestrial abominations will be released. These extra-terrestrials can then be released from their karmic chains, and ascend within their own evolutionary framework. This is a good example of the importance of the role of uncon-ditional love in the Sixth Root Race, and of how the older destructive patterns can be released and transformed into new beginnings, and new, more vibrant connections established. Compassion, love, understanding, and above all, a banishment and release of older encodements and fears, will help to lay the foundations for the galactic spread of the Sixth Root Race thought form.

Extra-Terrestrial DNA Frequencies

The new extra-terrestrial frequencies will be widely varied. Some will match the DNA frequency-vibrations already endemic to Earth and which were originally donated into the etheric and subtler matrices of Earth's development. These ancient DNA matrices and resonant light-frequencies will be re-activated through the re-emergence of the older extra-terrestrial connections. In bringing together these disparate aspects of DNA, firstly from the extra-terrestrial frequencies, and secondly from the DNA housed in your own physical bodies, there will be an awakening within the physical vehicles of the various planetary species. This awakening in terrestrial organisms and extra-terrestrial frequencies will lead to a massive outpouring of love and light. It will be a reuniting of DNA, and will represent a coming home in a very deep, energetic sense. It will be an old reunion of long-lost relatives. The divergence of inter-relationships will astonish you, and will open up new dimensions within your own awareness of who and what you really are.

There will also be a grouping of entirely new extra-terrestrial frequencies, new in the sense that these frequencies have not previously been associated with the Planet, and were not involved in the original donation of DNA into the etheric matrix. These new frequencies will present new opportunities for all light workers to build bridges into previously uncharted dimensions, and to swap experiences with these new extra-terrestrial friends.

The Devic Kingdom

The other main area where new frequency experiences and opportunities will be accessed is through the Devic Kingdom resident on your Planet. Devic life-forms are an alternate life-form which act as a binding force between matter and are present in a wide array. In all life, they act as the super glue which holds the cellular structure together. Devas are different from Elemental life-forms which inhabit plants, rocks, streams, lakes, the earth, and under-ground. Both the Devas and Elementals are opening up to the new frequencies entering the Planet. In particular, the Devas are readying themselves to vacate some of their old spaces, and to take up some of the areas soon to be made available by the upwardly-evolving human beings.

Communication with the Devic Kingdom presents another unique range of opportunities. Levels of expression that have lain dormant in the majority of you for many centuries will be reactivated. You have all evolved through the Devic Kingdom, and the increase in frequencies will present you with the means to communicate more simply and intuitively than before.

The Devic Kingdom has its own frequency array, which occupies a more specific range of planes than some of the other frequencies that you will encounter. These Devic frequencies will be extremely powerful. It will also help connect you with the elemental life-force present within the Planet, and also provide another opportunity for you to recapitulate your own older Devic frequencies. The recapitulation of the Sixth Root Race is not just about the older Root Races, but also about the spread of all life-forms, terrestrial and extra-terrestrial. It might be interesting to meditate on this point when the time feels appropriate.

The structural reality or thought form that is present within the Devic Kingdom is extremely important. We have spoken of raising the vibration of all sentient beings on the Planet, and the Devic Kingdom of minerals, plants, and animals is no exception. Collectively, the Devic Kingdom will seek to vibrate at a higher level, and this is partly what we meant earlier in saying that Devic life-forms will take up the spaces vacated by the human race. The Devic Kingdom is a collective kingdom, unified by the energy patterns of many different ray types[17] and their chosen paths up the evolutionary ladder.

Communicating with the Devic Kingdom

Two things stand out when we consider communication with the Devic Kingdom. The first is that we should actively seek to communicate with all Devic life-forms, thereby connecting with their sentient wisdom and love. The second is that the new credo of Sixth Root Race living is the establishment of a new level of information-flow. The crescendo of the collective energy impulse will establish a greater resonance between Devic life-forms and ourselves. This, in turn, will produce a substantial out-flowing of information and wisdom. As we ascend our frequency, so does the Devic Kingdom.

Think for a minute or two of the depth and splendour of the mountain vibrations, or the Devic energies contained within them. The force that unifies them is *love*. The Devic energies may not be consciously aware of this, but it is nonetheless so. As the frequencies ascend, the new vibrations will infuse the stones, rocks, and mountains, thereby raising the vibrational level of the Planet in a very direct way. As with all of you, there will be a stripping-away of older frequencies. This process can be clearly seen today through earth movements and extreme weather conditions. These are part of the overall process, during which the life-forms held within the Mineral Kingdom will begin to merge with the light, and to offer a new form of communication to those willing to receive it. This communication will be direct, through the heart, and will help each of you to recall the resonant frequencies of ages gone by, during your own evolutionary path, blazed through the Mineral Kingdom. This recapitulation is important, for in the communication and the communion, new bridges will be opened.

On one level, this will give people a deeper understanding of the significance of the Planet's new vibration. It will enable you to feel as one with the Earth; with mountains, meadows, planes, fields, streams; with trees and bushes. This will be a true communion of hearts. The term 'a heart of stone' will take on a dramatic new meaning. How can a stone have 'heart'? How can you connect with the source of Divine Love needed to support true physical expression? Or to put it another way, how do you connect with the energy inside which is an expression of the web of Divine Love which supports all life? It represents a different way to view the world and its land-masses, deserts, valleys, and continents. Each aspect has its own unique signature and representation of the physical.

In connecting with this new understanding, you will come to know what it means to live as one with the land, to live ever mindful of the multi-faceted Devic energies, and to connect through the heart with them. They provide another doorway to your evolution.

As you ponder your destiny, remember that your true connection is with Heaven and Earth, and that a true connection with Earth is a connection of the heart. This recognition of the heart is really necessary as a first step in anchoring the light into planet Earth. Once this anchoring has been achieved, you will better understand the damage that has been done to your Devic links; you have only to look around you to see the abuses that you are committing. Recognition and understanding of your deep connection with the Devic Kingdom will enable you to halt the process, to repair the links, and to restore the trust. You are about to assume responsibility as key-holders of your planet, and it is thus essential that the connections be re-established, and that then become pivotal to your way of life, rather than being smothered and ignored.

So look to your heart, connect with the land, and be open. The land will respond equally openly. Trust in this.

Invoking the Sixth Root Race Frequencies

The enormity, beauty and unity of this experiment are quite staggering. As you feel into the interplay of energies, recapitulations, and new connections, along with the blending of your energy fields and DNA frequencies, it should become apparent that the Sixth Root Race has another important feature. The manner in which you invoke these connections will impact directly the outcome. For example, invoking with an open heart, an empty mind, and with intent of purpose will be much more powerful than doing so for purely selfish purposes. The breadth and diversity of these invocations, when coupled with the frequency spread of the various life-forms, means that the Sixth Root Race frequency-vibration is entirely open-ended. It has the potential to occupy a huge spread of frequencies and connections, and to usher the glory of a new age of communication, merging, and divinity. The potential is utterly limitless — all is possible. So, we urge you to think seriously about this opportunity which encompasses such diversity and to realise that the Sixth Root Race is what humanity makes of it.

Frequency Chimes

Much has already been said about different frequencies, their origins, and their effects upon your systems. We are now going to look at how specific frequency-vibrations can interact and multiply with other frequencies. These interactions are known as frequency chimes. Frequency chimes represent the potential balancing of a group of frequencies associated with the release of older, stagnant energies. When a diverse array of frequencies come together, such as when a group of people meet with a common purpose, or when there is a connection with many different life-forms, there will usually be a representation of both discordant and harmonious vibrations. Through focus on the more harmonious frequencies, interesting things can happen: as they build up, rather like a series of harmonics, it is possible to establish a keying-in[18] frequency. This represents a negotiated access point to the diversity of frequencies present, and is something of a composite of the harmonic vibrations. Through this keying-in frequency it is then possible to generate a frequency chime which resonates through the hearts of many. Just as the keying-in frequency is like the key to a lock, so it is that the frequency chime is like the opening of the door: the doorway to a new resonant energy.

Frequency chimes can clear out, and open new frequencies extremely rapidly. Rather than clearing out one aspect of a past life at one point at a time, it is as if the collective unity of many different past lives, from many different people, can be cleared simultaneously. This is akin to clearing out old frequencies in a turbo-charged manner, i.e. much more powerfully and rapidly. This also gives a strong clue as to the importance of group work: only through group work can these frequency chimes be fully activated.

There is a second aspect to frequency chimes which involves connecting with the heart centre directly. Building up a resonant frequency between people's heart chakras makes it possible to use specific frequency rapports to 'blast open' the internal space of these heart centres. (Care needs to be taken in this process.) In circumstances where there is a perfect karmic blending and harmonic between members of a group, and where the older karmic ties of bondage have been substantially cleared, it is possible for the higher collective vibration of the group members to resonate in a perfect harmonic frequency. This will bring about a 'selfless' chime of true purity, true love, and true divinity. This is a rare occurrence, but one which is made possible by the coming of the Sixth Root Race.

If the overall love vibration within a group is high enough, it can be amplified and harmonised to produce a frequency chime which can create a portal or dimensional doorway of light that is akin to a giant heart chakra. The energy generated through such a frequency chime can then be used as deemed appropriate, and according to the highest dictates of Divine Intent.

These portals of love, of Divine Intent, will become more common as the Sixth Root Race becomes reality. Various groups across the globe are beginning to ready themselves for the induction of the new frequency chimes, and just as a single group can produce a frequency chime of pure love, so it is that different frequency chimes can merge and harmonise with others as they arise from other groups or collectives with pure intent. These frequency chimes will be the Divine Acorns which produce the woods and forests of the Sixth Root Race. They will be centres of extremely pure and high vibration, that will help to usher the expanding array of new frequencies into the Planet.

As these different groups connect and merge, so the Sixth Root Race frequency will ascend dramatically and majestically. On the inner planes there is intense excitement at this prospect.

Planetary Frequencies

Much is written in your popular culture about astrology, and the influences of various planets upon the human system, but the depth and, in particular, the spiritual essence of this ancient science is often lost. The rather parochial perspective placed by you upon planetary activities is also not especially conducive to the attainment of a deeper understanding of the various processes of cosmic vibration and inter-planetary vibrational energies. While it is appropriate to consider the effects of all the planets in your solar system, it should also be recognised that Earth has very deep inter-planetary exchanges with a number of other, more distant systems. Before discussing some of these, it is worth putting into perspective the relationship between Earth and some of her solar-system 'neighbours'.

Perhaps the most important planet in this respect is Mars. Although it is the closest planet, its long association with the human species has been lost in the mists of time, and has yet to be fully appreciated by the human race as a whole. The fact that there is discussion of a manned trip to Mars at this time is no accident, but what might be found there could be a profound shock to your collective psyche.

Prior to Earth colonisation, Mars was also inhabited, and had a climate, and a wealth of life not too dissimilar to those of Earth, although the degree of DNA cross-pollination or fertilisation from external sources was significantly less than on Earth. The Martian frequencies also accommodated a more masculine energy pulse, which contributed, in the end, to the destruction of life on that planet, and also to the total and irreversible destruction of any life-supporting, sustainable atmosphere.

It is not necessary to dwell on the 'whys' and 'wherefores' of this destruction, nor of the interactions with another group of extra-terrestrials, known as the Lyrans, at that time. What is of use today, in the resurgence of the new planetary frequencies, is that the destruction of life on Mars has a deep-rooted connection within the psyche of light workers, and of others who were involved in the original process of planetary colonisation. Consequently, just as some of the older Atlantean frequencies are being flushed out of your system at present, the same may also happen to the even older Martian frequencies which are held within your energy fields. There is, in relation to Martian mythology, a deep and unexplained pain or sadness connected with that planet's destruction, and as you connect with the older Atlantean vibrations, Martian memories may also re-awaken. This is nothing to be alarmed about, since it represents a further, deeper flushing-out of those old, slower frequencies.

While there have been older energetic associations with other planets in the solar system, in particular with Saturn and

Uranus, it is not necessary at this time to dwell upon these resonant vibrations, although as the energies escalate, the time will ultimately come when they will need to be flushed out.

Earth and Other Planetary Systems

What is more important at present is the need to connect with other planetary systems which reside outside of your solar system, but with which Earth has a strong frequency-rapport. There are five principle planetary systems involved, located within several different star systems. They are: Sirius, the Pleiades, Alcyone, Drago, and Lyra. Each of these planets has a different-frequency rapport with Earth. Some are more positive (lighter), and some more negative (darker). The main issue to be confronted over the next five years on Earth is the removal of some of the slower-frequency vibrations linked to the Pleiadian and Lyran planetary systems. In particular, there will be a battle — not in the conventional sense, but on the inner planes — of the choices presented between light and darkness. For as your frequencies ascend, so some of these older, slower frequencies will need to be stripped out and released. For many of you, this will require the removal of older fear frequencies associated with the reptilian energy that is connected with some of these systems. This energy is deeply embedded in many of you, and will need to be flushed to the surface and released. Much of this energy is housed in the lower centres, in particular the root, sexual, and solar plexus chakras.

As with the older frequencies from the Earth DNA lineage, the actions of calling in the group, connecting with the Paramatman Light, and sending these slower frequencies into It, will ensure their speedy and complete release. Their removal from your lower centres will enable a realignment and rebalancing of your higher centres. This will be especially important for your throat and third eye centres, which have been particularly held in check, or limited, by some of the older frequencies. This cleansing will be most beneficial to both centres, and the struggle that many light workers have experienced in their throat centres will begin to be alleviated. This will allow a return to a more balanced position within the overall functioning of your chakra systems.

Rebalancing Planetary and Solar System Karma

The removal of some of the older planetary frequencies will also play an important role in the rebalancing of the planetary and solar system karma. For just as there is individual, group, and planetary karma, so there is also solar system and galactic karma. Just as we each have to release the old karmic ties which bind us to the physical plane, so the Planet has to release its own karmic obligations, both within the solar system and with more distant parts of the Galaxy. Although an appreciation of *why* these karmic connections need to be released is beyond us, it is sufficient to know that this must take place as part of the Sixth Root Race programme of ascendancy.

The planetary energies that are being released through Earth's immersion in the wave of Photon Belt energy are of critical importance. This new energy wave will help to drive out some of the older planetary energy 'cysts' which have remained dormant. Again, this can be seen in the earth movements, dramatic weather patterns, and climatic shift, occurring all over the globe. One other factor that will have a major impact is the phenomenon of polar wandering[19] and geomagnetic reversal[20]. The North and South poles of the Planet have undergone geomagnetic reversals many, many times before, and at some point during the Sixth Root Race emergence, over the next 1,000 years, there is likely to be another. This will mark a completion and a rebalancing of the cycle linked to the old Atlantean frequencies.

Aside from geomagnetic shifts and polar wanderings, there will continue to be dramatic changes to Earth on the etheric and astral levels. As the substance of new mental frequencies is demanding that a new array of energies be accessed and illuminated, so the planetary heart-beat, in its continued increase in frequency, will have remarkable effects on all planetary life-forms. The love-vibration that will be transmitted through the planetary heart-beat will play a major role in activating the heart centres of all living creatures, and in those creatures which do not have well-formed heart centres, it will nonetheless contribute to their opening and expansion.

The increase in Earth's planetary pulse beat will have a divine impact on the other planets with which she has close karmic ties. The further ascendancy, in terms of both vibration and the removal of old karmic ties, will be dictated by this increase. Deeper planetary heart connections will be born, and this will be one of the ways in which the Sixth Root Race frequency-vibration will be spread, and shared with other planets and solar systems. A majestic rippling effect will take place throughout the Galaxy.

> It is the majesty and beauty of the Sixth Root Race plan, coupled with the involvement of such a multiplicity of dimensions, planes, planets, life-forms, and solar systems, which will be so staggering to you. You are not just involved in a local phenomenon. What happens on Earth will have karmic repercussions throughout the Galaxy. This is the grand plan, the Divine Plan. This is why light workers must be flexible, grounded, and committed to working with the massive diversity and array of new frequencies, karmic connections, and light-vibrations that will engulf their systems. This is the challenge, the call that has gone out to all light workers, the call that is now being answered on so many different levels, and in so many different ways. If one could connect with the perfection, the scale, and the beauty of this process, one indeed would be fully connected and merged with the Divine, with God the Beloved.

Chapter 5 • The Avataric Network

The Avatar of the Age

The Avataric Network or Avataric Frequencies, as they are known, represent the direct manifestation of the God-Head[1] or God-Force on Planet Earth. There is much debate over what constitutes an Avatar, and over whether or not certain Divine Beings truly are Avatars. For our purposes, an Avatar is defined as a direct incarnation of God on the Planet, and as One Who has assumed certain aspects of karma to enable Him to incarnate here. The role of the Avatar is to open up the new frequency-notes demanded by our future, and to map out the future destiny of all life on Earth. Avatars do not come for humankind alone; their role is to facilitate the awakening and emergence of Divine Consciousness in all living beings.

The Avatar of this Age is Meher Baba. The Avatar incarnates every 700 or 1400 years, depending upon the spiritual needs of the time. The Presence of the Avatar always heralds a major shift in the development of life, particularly for the human race. This can be seen very clearly through examination of some of the past Avatars. For example, the Christ initiated a dramatic shift in human consciousness, and a deeper understanding of Divine Love, although a great many of His teachings have been misinterpreted or restructured for political ends. The Prophet Mohammed manifested the energies that led to the decline of the Roman Empire in the 6th and 7th Centuries, and, later, to the Age of Reason. In earlier times, Lord Krishna manifested the relationship between war and peace more clearly. This is to name but three of the Avatars[2] of the past.

Meher Baba represents the culmination of all this work, and the Divine Plan, as set out by Him during His lifetime, covers the next 5,000 years. The physical Presence of Meher Baba, and His ongoing Work, are ushering in a new dawn for humankind, as evidenced by the emergence of the Sixth Root Race. During His Life Meher Baba said that He had come to awaken people, not to teach them. The Divine Love expressed by Him, and his Divine Compassion, have touched the heart of Baba lovers throughout the world. For Meher Baba and His followers, the awakening, in a direct sense, has to do with loving God as much as possible, and with learning to place this love for God, or Meher Baba, in its rightful place — at the centre of our lives.

The love and the light that are being pushed through by the Avataric Network form the most significant factor affecting Earth's vibration at this time. The current frequency shift was initiated during the Great War (the First World War), at the instigation of Shirdi Sai[3], or Sai Baba of Shirdi, as He was known. New doorways of light were opened as a result of the conflict, and these were instrumental in preparing the way for the new energies entering the Planet today. Sai Baba of Shirdi was one of five Perfect Masters who called the Avatar into physical incarnation. Shirdi Sai dropped His Body in 1918, shortly after the end of World War I. It is said that prior to doing so, He announced to His followers that He would take birth again eight years later, in southern India. On 23rd November, 1926, Sathyanarayana Raju was born to humble parents in an isolated village some one-hundred miles from Bangalore. He was a most unusual child, who at the age of fourteen announced Himself as the reincarnation of Sai Baba of Shirdi, thereafter becoming known as Sri Sathya Sai Baba. Sathya Sai Baba is overseeing many of the changes that are happening on the Planet.

Because this is an Avataric Age, there is an unprecedented open access to astral and mental light for all of Earth's life-forms. This is a time of marvellous opportunity for all light workers to be part of the great Mind of One experiment in raising the planetary frequency. This will be an ongoing process over many, many decades.

The Avataric Network is, in one sense, acting as a triangle of energy-distribution. This distribution is based firstly through Meher Baba, Who opened up the Planet more clearly to His true love-frequency; namely, *unconditional love*. The second aspect is brought through by Sathya Sai Baba Who reflects the clearing and cleansing of the Planet on all levels, through the removal and restructuring of old thought forms, and through much of the manifested clearance work from the fourth plane and below. The third pillar in this process is the open access to mental light and Paramatman Light. One direct way in which this is being manifested is through Mother Meera[4]. It should be recognised that although an Avatar will reflect all possible frequencies, He will emphasise specific aspects. The same is true, although in a slightly different way, for Perfect Masters and other Divine Beings. Each has a different area of emphasis or field of speciality.

Perfect Masters

The Avataric Network is facilitated and called into being by the Divine Will of the Perfect Masters. The Avatar does not have any choice in whether or not He incarnates since His Physical Presence is determined by the Perfect Masters. There are five Perfect Masters present on the Planet at any one time, three who work directly with humanity, and two who do not. An example of a Perfect Master today is shown through the Divine Expression of Ammachi, the Divine Mother[5]. Previous examples of Perfect Masters[6] have included John the Baptist, Zar-Zari-Zarbaksh, Hazrat Babajan, and Upasni Maharaj. Consequently, the role and emphasis of each of the Divine Beings, whether they be Avatars or Perfect Masters, are a source of great blessing to all humanity. To be blessed by an Avatar will lead to a significant benefit over many, many lifetimes.

It is not the purpose of this book to discuss the difference or relevance in spiritual terms of the respective roles of the Avatars or Perfect Masters. There is much that has been written on this subject already. However, what is relevant today, as part of the unlocking of the heart, is the realisation that each of us has the potential to connect with an Avatar or a Perfect Master, and to invoke that connection at all times. It is as if we can ring the doorbell of the Avatar's abode, and ask for an audience, or rather ask to be recognised, and to become more closely involved in the Divine Plan through Universal Work[7].

Connecting with an Avatar is a slow process, which develops over many, many ages, as each soul aspect ascends through the different planes of consciousness and inner experience. An Avatar will work on many levels; those within one's sphere of reality, and those outside of it. For example, on one level an Avatar will speed up your karma, while on another He will help you untie and realign areas of karmic difficulty in a more direct way.

The Avatar and Unconditional Love

An Avatar has many attributes, but above all else, an Avatar will show you *unconditional love*. For many people this notion is a difficult one to understand. Many view the love which they may lavish on their family, or nearest and dearest, as being unconditional, but this is very rarely the case, because unconditional love is just that: totally independent of events, circumstances, acts, words, or thoughts. In situations where a person feels somehow affected, emotionally or otherwise, by acts involving their loved ones, then their love is in fact conditional. It is only when it does not matter what that person does to you, and where you are not in any way **attached** to the outcome, that you can hope to attain in your heart a position of pure unconditional love.

Viewed from this perspective, it becomes clear that we can safely entrust ourselves to an Avatar's Divine (unconditional) love for us, because an Avatar will always act in a way which has our best interests at heart — on *all* levels, not just the physical. This means that through the unconditional love of the Avatar, we can begin to comprehend and integrate the love vibration being transmitted to us by Him. This is not a concept for the head. It is an experience for the heart.

What is essential as the Sixth Root Race emerges, then, is to connect with all your heart to an Avatar or a Perfect Master. At first this may seem difficult, but all you need to do is to ask for help to open up to the Avatar's love. It is rather like a baby beginning first to crawl, then to walk, and finally to run. Your initial connection with Him may not seem very strong, but you can ask to connect ever more strongly with the Avatar's Love. In time this connection will become deeper and more powerful, and it is, by definition, never-ending. Remember this, because although it is very simple, it is extremely important. As the energies increase in synchronicity with the planetary heart-beat, one way in which you can directly keep step is to invoke the love of the Avatar, to ask to be open, and to love the Avatar in return.

It is true that each individual will have a different connection with an Avatar or a Perfect Master, and that different Divine Beings may grace you with Their Presence during different periods of your life, or sometimes all at once. This is natural, and to be expected. Just as the Avatar's love is unconditional, so it is that the Spiritual Hierarchy works in concert, and that different Divine Beings will, therefore, work together. There are some who believe in only one Avatar, or one Perfect Master. This is a matter for their conscience, and for their evolving connection with the Divine. Each person will work with an Avatar or a Perfect Master in a way that is perfect for them. How could it be otherwise when the Divine is at work? As before, it is a case of letting go of the preconceptions of your mind, and allowing your heart to open to the Divine Frequencies and Love of the Avatars and Perfect Masters. This is what counts, and everything else that affects you in the three-dimensional world is really illusion. Divine Love, learning to be open to it, and ultimately to merge with it, is what will lead you back to your Source.

Connecting to the Divine Within

Why is this connection to Divine Love so important now? Put simply, it is because the planetary frequencies are opening up, and there is an unprecedented amount of Divine interest in

Planet Earth. This is what makes it a time of unique opportunity to connect with the Avatar of the Age, and with other Divine Members of the Spiritual Realms. In short, there exists an opportunity to have *direct* access to God, and not to have the Divine Frequencies stepped-down[8] through organised religions or through other means. It is the right of every living being to be able to connect with the divinity within themselves and to allow this to flow through. This is what the experiment embodied in the Sixth Root Race is all about. The key is to recognise your own divinity, to access it through your heart, and to expand the love and the light emanating from within yourself. Through invocation, by desire, by love from your heart, all of these things will be possible and you will discover who and what you truly are.

As you open your heart to the Divine, and as you connect with the Avataric Network, and with Divine Beings on many different levels, so it is that your perception of what is real and what is not real will be shattered. The veil of illusion will drop away, and a new dawn of light and love will emerge on the Planet. The key for all of you is to look inside your heart, and to seek to love the Divine, the Beloved, more and more. It is said that if you take one step towards the Avatar, He will take ten steps towards you. Ask and invoke. In doing this, as you build up your love for the Avatar, the Divine, it is possible for you to become at one with Him.

Meher Baba said that the aim and goal of life is as follows[9].

The Aim and Goal
The aim of life is to love God.
The goal of life is to become one with God.
To do this, you have not to renounce the world,
But to renounce low desires, dishonesty and hypocrisy.
Then in the midst of activities you will be loving God as He
 should be loved.

Sixth Root Race living is about having God at the centre of our life in a way that is meaningful for each of us. This is pivotal and in doing this, it will be that all flows from this. We shall be living life according to God's Will, and playing our part in the Universal Work according to God's Will.

> Building up this alignment with God's Will is incremental. As Meher Baba increasingly comes into your life, you will realise that He is not there enough, and so you will seek ways to bring Him in more and more. At first, the Avatar seems to be in your life to a small degree. Then this increases, and you start to feel that He is in your life more and more, until there is a point at which you cannot remember a time when He was not in your life. It is this 'love affair', between you and the Divine which should be at the centre of Sixth Root Race living; something that you earnestly strive towards. It is similar to climbing the highest mountain peak: this can be arduous, but when you reach the top, the view will be second to none. In the case of your connection to Divine Love, the experience of feeling God's love inside of you will be unlike anything that you will have encountered before.
>
> This love is the most rapid means by which your heart can be opened, and through which you can be released from the karmic ties that bind you. It will also ensure that you are in the right place at the right time, and living your life according to His Will.
>
> For some of you, this may be difficult to understand. This is not surprising, and it should not be regarded as a failure or a cause for criticism. It is just that each person is awakened to the inner Divine Love at a pre-appointed time. You don't find the Avatar, the Avatar finds you. Sometimes this is done in an exquisitely convoluted and beautiful way, to allow the opening of your heart to occur precisely, and according to His Will. At other times it may be more direct, but **always** according to His Will.

As with all things, you can ask to have the process speeded up. This may mean that the stripping away of older, slower frequencies is more robust, but the end result will be the same. It entails connecting with God's Love in your heart, and creating a space within your heart to be as open as possible to the Paramatman Light and Love. It requires opening your heart more and more, through invocation at all times, in all places, and in all circumstances. This is the promise that was made to many during the lifetime of the Christ, and this is the promise that is being fulfilled by the arrival and opening of the Sixth Root Race portal. This is the gift that is given. Take it, and run with it.

The Divine Fire

The Divine Love that is being channelled into the Planet at this time is unimaginable. We have spoken before of the battle that is taking place on the astral planes, and likened it to a series of hurricanes. If you were able to imagine the Divine Flame of God's Love bearing down on you, then it would be as an immense Sun, all-radiant, all-powerful, beaming into the space of all life-forms on the Planet. This Sun is opening up doorways of opportunity to the heart. As the Father's Fire enters your space, so the past will be banished, the ray of suffering upon which humanity has been for so long will be removed, and the ray of love will be activated on the time line of the Sixth Root Race.

The Divine Fire will flow into each of you, and will open up all your centres. It will burn away the old, and pave the way for the Divine swirl of liquid light and love to descend into your space from the Paramatman. The Paramatman will show you the Way, the Truth, and the Light: the light of lost opportunities rekindled for new awakenings, the light of Divine Intent and Divine Love to activate your cells and the spaces between your cells, so that the Divine Spark of immortality may grow within you. This does not mean the immortality of your physical vehicle, but the immortality of your soul, and your recognition and understanding of this fact. The seeds of love are being sown, and will be nurtured into full bloom by the Unspoken Word of Meher Baba. This has been foretold, and will come about according to the Divine Plan.

As the Father's Fire burns away the old and opens up the opportunity to bring in the new, so it is that the Divine Mother's love will soothe away the old pains, the old sufferings, and the old abysses. There will be many personal abysses to cross, but the one common abyss, that all must cross, is to acknowledge and trust their love of God.

Raising Your Vibration

The Avataric Network of frequencies provides a unique opportunity for all life-forms on Earth at this time. This is also an opportunity for the spiritual evolution of the human family in other planetary systems. In connecting with the Avatar, it is as if everything on one level has to be given up, offered up to the Avatar. For many of you, there will be a great deal of fear associated with this process. Some of you may not be welcoming this opportunity with open arms, and are standing around in trepidation at what may present itself around the next corner. Remember that what you invoke in a negative way will be reinforced by negative experiences. Should you choose to raise your vibration, and to focus on positive experiences, then this will be reflected in what is presented to you.

Part of the challenge of Sixth Root Race living is to raise your vibrational level to the highest that you can attain. There is a constant need to invoke the Avatar as part of this operation, to lift you above the negative substance of fear-based thought forms, and of slower-frequency thought forms generally, that would like to find a permanent resting place in a light worker. So whenever fear presents itself to you, remember that this is but a frequency, and that if you choose to rise above it, then you will not be affected by it. It is a case of being vigilant, and also of recognising that you are in the vanguard of this change. You must blaze a trail through these new frequencies, and find ways of moving through the slower-frequency energies which are so pervasive.

Much of what we have said about raising your vibration, connecting with your guides, invoking your divinity and bringing through the Paramatman Light is but preparation for the deeper and more resounding connection with the Avatar of the Age and His Divine Consort of Masters, and other Divine Beings. All of this has been perfectly orchestrated, and will unfold in a sublime way. However, it does require you to embrace the changes that are upon you with joy, and with a profound desire to serve the Divine in whatever way is deemed appropriate and necessary according to the Divine Plan.

It is important to note that none of this is about competition. Each one of us has a significant role to play in the changes that are now upon us. The spirit of competition — of who is, and who is not, fit or worthy to serve — is a slow-frequency energy. It is a thought form of the Fifth Root Race, and as such it has no place in our future and must, therefore, be discarded.

Emotional Detachment

A certain amount of emotional ruthlessness will be required. We have spoken of the need to use your emotions as doorways into your past, present, and future, but you must understand that the emotions will not lead you to your true self, in the spiritual sense. They will need to be balanced with situations and opportunities as these present themselves. For example, if a person is emotionally very unhappy, or having a difficult time, you may wish to empathise, to align yourself with that person. However,

£1-50

asiact

The Art & Science International
Academy of Colour Technologies

The AURA-SOMA®
Colour rose

Dev Aura, Little London, Tetford, Lincolnshire LN9 6QL UK
Tel. +44 (0)1507 533218 Fax. +44 (0)1507 534025
Email. info@asiact.org Web. www.asiact.org

Registered Charity No. 1063855

there is a strong case to be made for *acknowledging* his or her emotion, but not dropping your frequency to match theirs. Dropping your frequency will render you unable to help the person's process, because you will then be caught up in the same emotional turmoil. To the outsider this may seem rather cold, but in these times, when it is often regarded as a good thing to let the emotions flow freely, a certain balance has to be struck. Emotional over-indulgence is similar to a needle being stuck on a record player, and it does nothing to clear the energy at the source of the emotional disturbance.

Emotional detachment is a stance from which one acknowledges someone else's emotional situation, but without *colluding* in it. (It is, after all, better to throw a lifeline to someone struggling in the water, than to jump in after them, and risk finding yourself also overwhelmed by it.) One is then in a position to help that person, firstly to recognise the emotion for what it is, and then to release it.

Perfect Masters and Avatars use a similar process, although on a much grander scale, when helping their disciples to clear their sanskaras[10]. Emotions are drawn to the surface through interpersonal conflicts. As this happens, the opportunity arises for the disciple to see the emotion for what it is. This assistance is given from a position of unconditional love; for permitting someone to continue to be ruled by old emotional states does not constitute right action. Allowing them to connect with the pain of the emotion, and then providing the opportunity for clearing it, is an act of pure love. It is a service which the Avatars and Perfect Masters undertake continuously and selflessly. While the process is at times emotionally painful for the individual, an Avatar provides an unprecedented opportunity to clear his or her sanskaras.

For many people, any opening of the heart will involve clearing the solar plexus chakra, and old sanskaras. Other aspects of Sixth Root Race development, all of which are controlled by the Avatar, concern the unfolding of the heart vibration to match that of the Planet, and the opening of the third eye (brow) chakra. This latter opening will allow the new vibrations to register within your psyche.

The New Chakra System

Much has been written about the new chakra systems, and the plethora of new chakras that may or may not develop as the Sixth Root Race emerges. Part of the unification process concerns the balancing of all the chakras, and before new chakras can be opened under the Divine Guidance of Avataric Intent, there has to be a balancing of the old ones so that the new building-blocks can be introduced safely and effectively.

For many adepts[11], the goal in the past has been to unravel the kundalini[12], and to allow this particular divine vibration to rise from the spinal-base centre up to the third eye, and ultimately to the crown centre. This remains so, but it is tempered through re-balancing and the recognition that as the Paramatman Light is now invoked through the crown into the heart, and ultimately down into the lower centres, then there is a dual pattern of energy at work. This is nothing less than the fusion of the uprising kundalini energy with the downloading Paramatman Light. There needs to be a perfect balance within the seven chakras that are currently operating if this fusion of energies is to take place safely and effectively, and in a manner which will enable all light workers to remain grounded within the Planetary spindle of earthing energies.

It is this combination of the rising kundalini with the descending Paramatman Light which will drive the etheric, astral, and ultimately, the mental consciousness of the human race into its future divine understanding and interplay of energies. This balancing and blending will also set up the internal grid pattern or template for the establishment of a new series of chakra centres to be formed: an additional five centres, to be precise. Although there are some precursors of these centres known to you at this time, there will be several new ones which will be opened from the inner planes, and through the Divine inspiration of the Avataric Agency. It is appropriate to mention two of these at this time.

The Group Heart Chakra

The first chakra centre is the secondary heart chakra, which is located at the thymus gland, just below the manubrium point at the top of the sternum. The thymus gland produces T-lymphocyte cells up to the age of eight. After that it shrivels in size, and in adults is much smaller. However, as the new energies come in, and again are stimulated by the Paramatman Light, the thymus gland of old will be repositioned to accept more and more of It. This focal point, through its intimate connection with the heart centre, will allow the creation of a new, deeper heart centre, that will resonate with the collective and divine love of the group. So: your main heart centre will function as the primary doorway to your own divinity. Then, since the emergent Sixth Root Race demands the establishment of a *group* pulse, echoing *group* love, this secondary heart centre will act as a focal point for the new, *collective* heart frequencies, which will be a feature of the Sixth Root Race, and which will assist in raising the vibrations of all of Earth's life forms.

With the Paramatman Light feeding the emergent heart centre, our collective awareness of the Divine Matrix within us will be raised, allowing the collective light of Divine Love to shine through the portals of the new chakra. This will be the opening of a new gateway to the inner planes and beyond, a gateway which will permit the human family to resonate as a group, on a Divine Frequency that will resound through countless universes. We shall emerge from our 'chrysalises' of

Divine Intent into the light of collective love and collective responsibility. Consequently, the frequency rapport that will be demanded of the new heart centre will have a profound significance for the emergence of the Sixth Root Race.

Restructuring the Third Eye

The second chakra that will be heavily reactivated during the coming years is the third eye. Although this represents one of the 'original' chakras, it will evolve into a more complex *system* of chakras. Before going into this in more detail, some understanding of the different glandular systems around this area is needed.

Four structures impact directly upon the third eye. The first is the crown chakra, which has traditionally been understood as a connection with the 'Higher Self', with our Divine Self, or with the higher-frequency rapport that is established with the inner planes. The crown chakra also reflects the sum total of all the other existing chakras in the body, so where there is an imbalance in any other chakra, this will be reflected in the crown chakra. The Paramatman Light, as has already been mentioned, enters directly through the crown chakra.

The second point, etherically significant, is the ajna centre inside the back of the head, just by the medulla oblongata[13]. This is not always recognised as a chakra point, but it is in reality a key point in all light workers, since it represents the point of contact with our guides on the inner planes. The development of the ajna centre, and its expansion to house the frequency rapport that we need to establish with our guides, is essential at this time. In many light workers the ajna centre is underdeveloped, is too tight, and is often traumatised from past-life experiences. An important aspect of energy and healing work is to rebalance this centre, and to realign it with the intent of the heart centre and the throat or 'will' centre. Significant clearing of the throat centre is usually needed to accompany the opening of the ajna centre.

Two other physical points need to be considered. The first is the pituitary gland, which is housed in the sphenoid bone[14]. The sphenoid forms part of the floor of the brain. The pituitary is involved with the hormonal balance of the whole body, through the various pituitary hormones that are released. Over and above this physical process, the pituitary gland has a key etheric role in the distribution of pranic energy throughout the body. It also plays an important part in anchoring and distributing Paramatman Light to the other centres of the body. It is because the pituitary gland is so intimately connected with many other glands in the body[15] that it is one of the first points of activation by the Paramatman Light and of the subsequent activation, by association, of the other glandular centres of the body. Many people are experiencing substantial difficulties with their third eyes and pituitary glands, and often fail to recognise the 'knock-on' effects of imbalances in these two centres.

The final point of importance concerns the pineal gland[16], which is traditionally linked to the third eye, and in some cultures is regarded as the point of origin within the etheric of the third eye. While this is partially true, and the origins of this gland do concern light, the role of the pineal is also important in the distribution of light and dark frequencies within the substance of mind. The pineal gland today represents an incipient storage point for the Paramatman Light, and a point of activation for the restructuring of the third eye which is beginning to take place in many light workers. The pineal gland is also associated with sleep patterns. The irregular sleep that many people are experiencing, can be linked to the progressive activation of this gland by the Paramatman.

I would like to introduce the concept that the third eye, and its activation, are part of the rebalancing of a five-pointed star[17] structure. This structure takes in the ajna centre at the back of the head, the pineal gland in the centre of the head, the pituitary gland on the floor of the brain, the crown centre at the top of the head, and the third eye itself. It is not a structure in the physical sense, but more within the etheric, and the importance of the five-pointed star is that it represents a point of universal balance and harmony. As the structures mentioned above start to come into a greater balance with each other, then the third eye will begin to open, and to give greater access to numerous different levels for light workers.

It is also worth mentioning the importance of the throat chakra in this process; so much intent, both physical and etheric, is housed here. It is a precondition of the opening of the third eye that this chakra be opened and cleared through the procedures mentioned in earlier chapters. Any imbalances in the throat chakra will ultimately distort the symbolic balance of the five-pointed star.

Opening the Third Eye

The restructuring of the third eye can only occur through the inner planes, and again from authority within that realm. To forcibly open the third eye is a mistake, and can have negative consequences for the overall balance and well-being of one's physical vehicle. While the opening of the third eye is an essential process in Sixth Root Race evolution, it is the overlaying of this structure with a new fabric of intent that will be so important. It is as if the old structure of the third eye will be taken and upgraded in many different ways. It will also be sub-divided into two further structures, which will then provide the basis for a triple component third eye, if you like.

The third eye will process in many different ways the incoming electromagnetic frequencies of new vibrations. This will manifest differently for each individual, and, while it will open up clairvoyant capabilities for many people, the intent, format and arrangement of these new capabilities will vary from individual to individual. It will be a question of how the new frequencies on the inner planes are perceived. This process will be overseen by the Avataric Agency, and will require a significant and precise series of scientific adjustments over a period of time.

The three sub-divisions of the third eye will relate to different band-widths of intent, and different frequency vibrations. Full capacity in each of these sub-centres will vary from person to person, and will depend upon their intent and their sphere of operation. While the sub-divisions relate to aspects of visual range, the term as used here does not really fall within the traditional meaning of the word 'visual': intuition will play its part. The three sub-divisions or aspects may be likened to the intent shown on the physical and etheric, the astral, and the mental planes. Your third eye will reflect your activities within each of these areas.

The degree of importance of each of these new capacities, and the respective degree of opening required, will be determined by each individual's intent and inner-plane work. The key to this process is to be without expectation. Such judgements or predispositions will only colour the reality of the situation. Consequently, sensing and interpreting information received through the new frequency-vibrations that will be built into the subtler vehicles of all light workers, will be a painstaking and slow process. The watchword here is **preparation**: slow and strong growth is to be preferred to rapid and ragged growth which will be unable, in the long run, to support the diversity of frequencies that will be required within the biological vehicle of all light workers. Consequently, the third eye and its opening are very tightly controlled on the inner planes, and are an integral part of the Avataric Programme. The massive scope of the work undertaken by Sai Baba in His Divine Mission will be a key connection for many people in this respect.

The situation is similar to having a new computer, both in terms of hardware and software. The hardware relates to the structural changes within the physical, etheric, and other bodies, while the software relates to the information matrix or programme for recognising and interpreting the frequency impressions received by the individual. Both aspects need to be downloaded into the brain, turned on, and operationally tested, just as with a normal computer. The limits of operation, and understanding what the computer can and cannot do, are essential. Of necessity, this is a precision process that requires trust, patience, and care.

This sense of discovering one's new capacities will never be as we imagine it to be, and it is, therefore, best not to prejudge: just trust, invoke, and connect as deeply as possible. Many, many beings will be facilitating this process. Just as the Divine Intent of the Avatar is set upon the human form, so it is that the new centres and their opening will be dictated and invoked through our love of the Avatar and the Divine Hierarchy of Spiritual Masters. Holding this intent within our hearts, both individually and collectively, will help the awakening process, during which there will always be surprises, and ultimately an intense deepening of the way in which humanity understands itself. This understanding will encompass humanity's origins and its destiny, and how love for the Avatar is but a natural state for all of us.

Group Chakras as Dimensional Doorways

The Avataric Frequency, as it musters the new vibrations beneath its wings of Intent, will allow love and light to shine forth on to the Planet. This is so written, and will be followed through according to the Divine Plan. These frequencies will open up the new chakra points of intent, within your physical and etheric vehicles. At the same time, larger chakra points will be formed by the coming-together of groups of light workers, creating dimensional doorways of exquisite intent, and allowing communication with the new energies and Divine Beings on the inner planes. This too has been foretold. These new 'chakric' beacons will be bridges for the Sixth Root Race; bridges of Divine Intent, that will help to anchor the higher light frequencies into the Planet.

The vibrational 'suite' of new frequencies carried by this Avataric wave of Intent will be the culmination of all that has gone before, all that is presently in the Planet, and all that is to come. It is rather like the expansion of what is known, in cosmic terms, as a point singularity[18]; like unravelling and opening up a point of light that contains within it all the frequency accords of the past, present, and future. Then can the exquisite frequency-crescendo of Sixth Root Race living be released for all to connect with, for all to experience within their own multi-dimensional perspective. This is such a wondrous prospect, and the preparation that will be laid down over the next thirty years or so will serve to anchor the intent of this point singularity within your consciousness. And this is just the beginning.

Accessing the Informational Matrix of Light

While it is impossible to know the Divine Intent of the Avatar, there is some knowledge that can be accessed. For many light workers the key to divining high-frequency information lies in accessing the frequency intent and rapport of the informational matrix of light that is stepped directly down from the Avatar. This access is very much open-ended. light workers can either access the upper end of the spectrum, the lower end, or the middle portions, depending upon which plane level they are operating from. Information accessed at a lower plane level will obviously have become diluted during the descent from its original source, while information accessed from the higher planes will contain a more concentrated mix of frequencies. The reliability or veracity of the information accessed will be correlated with the part of the spectrum that is accessed. The key is to invoke the ascension of your frequency intent to the fullest extent. As this develops over time, a baseline position of strength should become established, which will allow access to the higher frequencies. From this vantage point the matrix of information and light that can be accepted will build daily. This means that the quality of information that can be accessed will improve.

Thus, while we see that for many people there remain issues over conflicting channelled information, the conflict is, in reality, a measure of the different levels that are being accessed. While there may be differences in the information that is channelled, what is of importance is that as the higher mental frequencies are accepted, so the true geometry of the information, in all its facets, can be accessed. The apparent discrepancies will then be recognised as part of a more complete picture. Accessing the higher mental frequencies will give greater clarity of information and light, which will reveal the true essence of Divine Intent. Just as there is a broad diversity of life on this Planet, there will also be a very broad array of different types of information that will be promulgated by a variety of sources. There will be a deluge of this and it will be very easy for light workers to become swamped. The key lies in remaining centered, in ascertaining the precise frequency-rapport of the information, and in psychometrising[19] the plane level[20], from where it is sourced. For example, some channellings refer to the destruction of the Planet, and ignore the laws of karma. Such information is sourced from the lower planes.

It is said that there will be seventy-seven false avatars, all claiming to be of Avataric status. Great care is needed to ensure that we are not taken in by these claims, nor by the people who promulgate them. The informational matrix that these 'avatars' claim to bring through will be of an extremely low vibration by comparison with the true Divine Avataric Intent that is manifested through the Paramatman Light. Learning to distinguish between these different frequencies will be of vital importance.

> By cultivating the connection with the Paramatman Light, you will come to know, within every fibre of your being, what is the nature of true Avataric Intent, as compared with what others may claim to be. This is not a collective issue in the sense that you should be persuaded by what others may say or think. Rather, it is a matter for *you* to ascertain: *feel* the Avatar in your

heart. Nothing else will do. Nothing else will suffice. This will be the ultimate test, in the sense of your knowing what you are, and where your true connections lie.

So: exercise discrimination, connect with your heart, and allow the Divine Love that is your birthright to flow into every fibre of your being. This will be the surest way to ensure that you connect, at all times, with the Divine.

The New Matrix Thought Form

We have looked at the resurrection of the chakra system within humankind, and how this will develop in the future. Of equal importance is an understanding of the new frequency thought forms which will be anchored into the minds and hearts of all who wish to ascend into the Sixth Root Race frequency.

Our starting point for all of this is the old occult[21] maxim that 'energy follows thought'. On one level this is extremely simple, yet tremendously powerful. On another, more practical, level, it is extremely complex, given the substance of mind, and the mind inter-relationships that currently undermine the human race: if energy follows thought, then as you *think* so your energy is coloured by the quality of the thoughts.

Every thought has a frequency, a vibration of intent. These can be manifested into the physical by the strength of the emotional matrix supporting the intent, or they can remain within the astral planes, where the energies are played out in a slightly different way. What has been said before about the storm that is raging in the astral planes is extremely relevant, and maintaining your vibrational intent and balance during this storm over the next ten to twelve years will be crucial. This cannot be over-emphasised, because your survival will depend upon it. There will be many who will drown within this maelstrom of astral frequencies, through being fooled by the quality of thoughts coming into their space.

What is needed, what is *demanded* by the Avataric Network, is the crystallization of a new matrix of thought forms, which will surpass and supersede the rather dismal array of those enshrined in the Fifth Root Race. This matrix will be a crystalline thought form of intent; a thought form that vibrates at such a high frequency of light and love, that it represents the blueprint for the Sixth Root Race, which as we have seen, is a thought form which is currently being called into being, primarily by the Avatar, secondly by the Spiritual Hierarchy, and thirdly by the light workers or Mind of One currently on the Planet. The new, crystalline matrix thought form will be directly connected to that of the Sixth Root Race.

So, the Sixth Root Race thought form starts off as a call for all light workers. Once this has been anchored into the awareness and substance of mind of all light workers, the thought form evolves into a call for pure mental light, combined with a deep connection with the Avataric Network and the Paramatman Light. Ultimately, once this thought form has induced a quantum shift in the vibrational intent of all living beings on the Planet, then it is time for the *substance* of this call to come into play. This *substance* is the new matrix thought form, the new crystalline structure of intent.

The Crystalline Matrix Thought Form

This crystalline thought form will represent the highest frequency-connection that will be attainable by the Sixth Root Race. It represents the highest mental imprint of light and information for Sixth Root Race living, and, as such, will deliver and enshrine a quality of light which has never been seen on the Planet before. It is worth considering for a moment why this thought form is (a) crystalline and (b) a matrix.

Crucially, the crystalline nature of our essence represents a deep-rooted connection with the Divine, crystalline energy being one of the highest-frequency mediums for anchoring the light into the physical.

As a component of the new frequencies, the Crystal Skulls will play an important role: representations from the mental planes will be manifested and anchored into the Planet through their physical presence.

It is said that there are twelve of them[22] in all, although an additional, 'key' Skull is required to open up a new dimension and panoply of light frequencies. This brings the hypothetical total to thirteen. Once all of these Skulls have been found and accessed, then the time for initiating this new matrix of intent will be upon us. The Crystal Skulls could, therefore, be said to represent a physical expression of this new crystalline thought form of the Sixth Root Race.

The question concerning the matrix should also be clarified. The matrix will allow a diversity of higher mental frequencies to enter the Planet. It will represent, much like the collective consciousness of the Mind of One, the means to host the vast array of crystalline thought forms that are needed. The matrix is similar to a multi-faceted crystal, although in this case the individual facets of the matrix convey specific frequency-vibrations of intent. This is why the *crystalline* substance of the Sixth Root Race is so important. It is also why all light workers need to raise their frequencies to connect with a wave harmonic of **collective** intent.

It is extremely difficult to do justice to the beauty, exquisiteness, and power of Divine Intent as expressed through this realisation of the crystalline thought form matrix. The full potential will only become clearer when you have raised your frequencies to a much higher threshold, and when the Sixth

Root Race thought form is initially anchored into your consciousness on a collective level. This is still some years away.

Realising Our Crystalline Heritage

The new matrix thought form will be initiated in the higher mental planes, and has as its Source the Divine Will of the Avatar of the Age. It will bring about a tremendous transformation in the astral planes, especially the higher ones. This, in turn, will be reflected in the lower astral planes, and within the etheric and physical vehicles of all living beings. The crystalline intent housed within the thought form will open new doorways to our realisation of our true crystalline nature.

> It is rather like being composed of liquid crystal that has, as its components, crystals of light and love. Each of these crystals has been impregnated with the highest frequencies available from the mental planes. The resultant connection and power manifested through Divine Love will be stupendous, and will link each of you into the Divine Plan and Network in an unprecedented way. It will be as if all the physical and subtle anatomy of each of you will be totally overhauled, and replaced by state-of-the-art crystalline 'lighting equipment'.
>
> The crystalline matrix, which will drive the frequency thought form of the Sixth Root Race ever higher, will superimpose the initial blueprint of the Sixth Root Race with a new, turbo-charged, structural one. This will be composed of pure light and crystalline energy that will have, at its very core, the Divine Manifestation of Unconditional Love, and the associated interplay of light frequencies. This crystalline thought form will flood the astral planes, and will represent a culmination and completion of all the clearing work that will have gone on in the years before. Added to the qualities mentioned above, it goes without saying that this thought form will be spectacularly beautiful in its inception.

Hopefully the foregoing gives an impression of what the new thought form will be like. As the years pass, the sense of impending advent of this new thought form will help to raise the frequency-vibration of Earth as a whole. Viewed overall, the advent will become more apparent once the storms on the astral and physical planes have subsided, and the Sixth Root Race thought form has become a physical reality. Only then will this new, directed beam of crystalline light and love be targeted into the space of the Sixth Root Race. Only then will the pioneers of the Sixth Root Race be able to hold this new vibration within their internal and external space.

> In conclusion, the Avataric Frequencies will drive the vibration of the Planet up at a very rapid rate. These Frequencies will seed into the astral and physical planes directed beams of light and love that will initially generate substantial change and turmoil. Following this cosmic cleansing process, a new dimension of space and intent will be present. It will allow a new frequency of light to drive the beginnings of the Sixth Root Race up to what may be termed its standard operating frequency. This process will take some seventy years in all, and will coincide with the hundredth-year anniversary of the physical death of Meher Baba. At this future point, the balance of light and dark on the Planet will have been reversed. Light will be represented as seventy-five percent of the totality of frequencies, as opposed to the present-day level of twenty-five percent. There is much to be done.

Chapter 6 • Frequencies of the Heart

Ascending Love-Frequencies of the Heart

All that has been described thus far can be summarised by the following phrase: 'ascending love-frequencies of the heart'. This encompasses, in a simple and direct way, the emergence of the Sixth Root Race: the placing of everything in our heart; the offering of our heart to the Divine; and the quest to be aligned with our heart, and that of the Divine, at all times. As we embody this, become this; then we become the Sixth Root Race, and express ourselves in Sixth Root Race living. This is a simple, central axiom of intent and experience.

When people think of new dawns and new beginnings, they are invariably drawn to the notion of physical changes and occurrences, rather than to changes of heart. It is only when our hearts are placed in the centre of our experience, in the centre of our life, that we shall see the paucity and limitation of using a physical reference-point to assess or define change. This is especially true of the Sixth Root Race, which is all about frequency, vibration, intent, and above all, about love in its many guises. In the latter respect, the Sixth Root Race particularly focuses on the ultimate form of love, which is Divine Love. In the final analysis nothing else matters, and nothing else, when it is considered across the aeons of time, has any lasting value.

> Once you realise that all the pasts, the presents, and the futures are ultimately invoked through love, and your wish to connect with pure Divine Love, then you will see that nothing else matters.
>
> There are many, many ways to God. God can be found in the blade of grass, in the sparkling sunlight on a dewy morning, or in the unconditional love of one beggar for another. All of these things are expressions of God's Love. The Sixth Root Race is part of this Divine Experiment. It is showing humankind the

way towards Him; how to connect with Him more; the way to love Him; how to love Him more and more; and how to bring Him more and more into your lives, into your hearts, in a permanent way.

The most important frequency of the heart is His Frequency of the Heart. His Frequency encompasses all the frequencies of Divine Love, Divine Compassion, and Divine Knowledge. We say to each of you, as you are called by Him, as you are invited to open your hearts to His Divinity and Love: recognise this great gift and the opportunity to feel Him inside you. You do not need any physical form to do this, for the only way is through your heart energy. Meher Baba will take care of the rest.

There is much in this that will be difficult to absorb at first, but do not be put off by this difficulty. The Divine spark, once ignited, will continue to burn steadily, constantly, and in proportion to what you invoke. In years to come, when you look back at these times, you will see how very far you have travelled. You may realise how the veil of illusion has been removed, and how you have turned your life around one-hundred-and-eighty degrees to face the love of the Divine Father. It will be through His Love, His Grace, that you will have succeeded in this. There is nothing to worry about. All will unfold according to plan; according to The Plan.

Divine Nomads

Many of you may have experienced a 'nomadic' existence. Your heart has been wandering through the mists of time, seeking the one true connection, the perfect alignment with the Divine Father. The emergence of the Sixth Root Race now provides you with the opportunity to connect with Him, and to move away from this nomadic existence of the heart. You can find your resting place, your true home. Home is where the heart is, home is where your true expression of Divinity can come through, and where your true connection and destiny lie. So the time of great wanderings in the desert and in the swamps, in isolation, is now over, as the group frequency calls you to face your destiny, in perfect alignment with the Father's Will.

The frequencies of your heart, which will call you to this point, to this ending and new beginning, will be specifically encoded from ages past, and according to your current contract on the Planet. While the process can be speeded up, it is nonetheless true that you will receive the call, although it may seem that you are the one doing the searching. It was ever thus with the Divine Father. As you connect with Him, and begin to come home into your heart, you will feel or sense new frequencies being activated within your heart centre. The seeds of these frequencies have been lying dormant for many, many years, and so it will seem as if you knew something all along, but could not remember it. As these new frequencies of Divine Love become activated, you may start to recall the times when they were initially laid down in your heart. You may realise that you have been through many lifetimes searching for the Divine, in connection with different Perfect Masters and Avatars from ages gone by. For example, you may sense a deep connection with the Buddha, or with the Christ, or with the immortal Babaji. This re-awakening of the ancient connection within your heart will be powerful, and consuming in the extreme. You will begin to glimpse, on a much grander scale, your true destiny, and your true route to connecting with God, the Divine. This will all come to pass.

While some of this may sound daunting or unlikely, there is no need to be afraid of failure. Do not fear that you may not be able to access these new frequencies. As you invoke them, as you call the Divine into your life at all times, so shall these seeds open up within your heart, and begin to grow into young saplings. In turn, the saplings will grow into strong trees, with roots that anchor your awareness into the Ocean of Divine Love. This again has been promised.

Determining Your Future

There has always been a need for people to feel secure in the future, safe in the knowledge that nothing will ever really change, and that they will be looked after. This older, non-dynamic view has to be dismantled, and this process really has to take place in our heart. The heart does not seek out stagnation, or closing down to new opportunities. The heart needs to soar, to sing, and to seek alignment with the new heights of frequencies that are coming into the Planet. This can only be achieved by allowing change into our heart and into our life, and trusting that the future will unfold in a perfect way, according to the Divine Plan and Greatest Good. There is no other way to approach the future. The worries of today are always resolved in the never-ending tomorrows, and if we worry all the time about the future, about something which has to yet to manifest in our space and awareness, then we are, by definition, limiting this experience, this unfolding.

The collective future is in your hands, and needs to be invoked at all times. As has been said before, the unfolding of the Sixth Root Race will depend upon the invocation of the highest frequencies of love and light into your space, and the subsequent anchoring of these twin flames into the Earth. This is the best way to determine the future; to open it to its greatest potential, greatest excitement, and greatest love. All else is secondary.

Feel the need for love in your heart, and feel the need for this to become a reality in the present and the future. Feel how empty and barren your heart has been in the past: how the connection that you have with it is something of a pretence; how it could be much deeper, and how it could be filled with the twin frequencies of love and light, as unified through the Paramatman Light.

The Great Invocation

Love and light can also be accessed through what is known as the Great Invocation[1]. The Great Invocation was seeded into the Planet by the Spiritual Hierarchy over fifty years ago. It was part of the preparation for what was to be at that time, and in many ways for what is still to come. The frequencies of Love and Light, which it represents and manifests, are the tuning-fork for the emergence of the Sixth Root Race. If you work with the Great Invocation, then you align yourself with God. You will also be aligning yourself in a different way, through invoking the future that has been promised, and which is now urgently demanded on the Planet. The Great Invocation runs as follows:

The Great Invocation

From the point of Light within the Mind of God,
Let Light stream forth into the minds of men.
Let Light descend on Earth.
From the point of Love within the Heart of God,
Let Love stream forth into the hearts of men.
May Christ return to Earth.
From the Centre where the Will of God is known,
Let purpose guide the little wills of men —
The purpose which the Masters know and serve.
From the centre which we call the Race of Men,
Let the Plan of Love and Light work out,
And may it seal the door where evil dwells.
Let Light and Love and Power restore the Plan on Earth.

So work with this Invocation in your heart, and open yourself to its true alignment, since the frequencies encoded within it will also activate seeds in your heart — seeds that are now ready to germinate and grow.

Heart Frequencies of the Sixth Root Race

The heart frequencies that will be activated by the emergence of the Sixth Root Race will have a number of very special and specific characteristics. We have spoken of the two heart chakras, and of the emergence of a new, collective heart vibration that will be anchored into planet Earth. This collective frequency will form the beacon for the emerging role of guardianship of · the Planet, and will also represent a frequency rapport for all other life-forms, both terrestrial and extra-terrestrial. This group love frequency has been very difficult for many to access in the past. Part of the problem has been the wash of old karmic frequencies from Atlantean, and subsequent, times, although the vibration on the Planet has not been high enough before to support this new level of collective love — which is an important point to remember.

The opening of this collective frequency requires special consideration. Think about the possibility of a collective harmonic of love and light which binds many people together. It is not that you necessarily have to know these people in an intimate way, but rather that the keying-in mechanism that you will all have, will represent a doorway of communication. The keying-in mechanism will be a recognition signal that each of you will recognise in the other. You may not be consciously aware of it at first, although your aura or subtler bodies will reflect it. It will be a more direct and specific recognition of the love and the divinity that are inherent within each of you. It will mean that you do not prejudge people with your minds in the way that you do now, but rather that you will connect with your hearts. Your heart will emit the Sixth Root Race frequency-vibration, and will allow you to connect more deeply, heart to heart, on an ongoing basis.

This, in essence, is what recognising and connecting with your divinity is about. It concentrates on the heart connection, on an inner understanding that makes no judgements about race, colour, or creed. It is a connection that recognises and accepts the divinity inherent within each and every one. So, as the heart chakras develop and expand within each of you, this new vibration will begin to 'kick in'. At first this will be only occasionally, but then more and more frequently, until it is with you at all times. This will take at least twenty years to be achieved.

When we speak of frequencies of the heart, we are not only referring to new seeds being planted within your heart, nor to their transformation into vibrant young plants. We are also indicating the recognition of these features in your fellow human beings, and in all other creatures and life-forms that are now gracing Earth. Sixth Root Race members will recognise that all are linked, that all are one, that all come from the same place, the Divine Ocean, and that ultimately all will return there.

There will also be a deep understanding that we are all extremely diverse within each species, as well as between different species, and that the Divine Spark of Love and Light is what truly unifies this diversity into the One. So, if a calamity strikes one part of the Planet, then we are *all* affected by this event. Another way of looking at it is to recognise that as all of our frequencies ascend, then so will the Planet's frequency ascend, and simultaneously. Through this collective unification of higher frequencies, it will become possible to access the Intent and Love of the Divine much more directly. This will be very much a homecoming for all life-forms on the Planet.

Gateways to Love

It should be clear by now that the heart is the main gateway to the highest love frequencies and light frequencies that are accessible to physical beings on the Planet. To talk of a gateway to love is an important thing, because it highlights the need, for all of us, to build gateways in our hearts to the new frequencies that are demanded of us today. To invoke love and light is the most powerful thing that we can do to help raise our frequency-vibration, that of our fellow human beings, and that of our Planet. But for many people, this straightforward act of invocation is often not trusted, or is ignored when circumstances demand it. This can no longer apply to light workers, who now need to concentrate on bringing their heart connections into all that they do, to build consciously a bridge from the heart to the highest accessible frequencies on the inner planes, and to use this bridge to allow a greater profusion of frequency-signals to come through to them, while at the same time enhancing the clarity of such signals.

These frequency bridges are two-way, and can be expanded and continuously built up. This is what needs to be acknowledged and accepted: that once the frequencies of the heart have been opened up they need to remain open, and that throughout physical incarnation the higher frequencies need to be continuously invoked.

There are no limits to the new frequencies of the heart and they will continue to build over the next one hundred years or so. We have spoken earlier about the pulse beat or heart-beat of the Planet, and of how the signature or keynote of all living beings will be taken from this heart-beat. As you anchor the light into the Earth, this will help to push up the frequency-vibration of the Planet. It is a two-way thing. As the Earth's vibration increases, so it is that the heart centres of all living beings are forced to register this change, and to adapt to it. Through this adaptation more light is called in, and earthed into the Planet. This, in turn, drives up the frequency-vibration still more. So it is that there are no limits to this process. It is entirely open-ended as to how much love and light are brought into the Planet.

Segregating the Frequencies

Now there are those, and there are many of them, who would like to see this change kept to a minimum; who would like the vibration of the Planet to remain anchored into the lower centres of your collective awareness and consciousness. There will be many times during this process when it will seem very difficult to raise the vibration, and that there is no point to this exercise. This is all an illusion. The truth of the matter is that as you invoke these higher light-vibrations, the slower frequency-vibrations of hatred, greed, abuse, and ritual destruction of life will be segregated. By invoking the higher frequencies of love and light, it will be possible to anchor yourself 'above' these slower frequencies, to overcome and to ride 'above' the predominant frequencies of fear and mistrust.

This will have several, very significant effects. Firstly, it will mean that those who would wish to pull your vibration down, for whatever reason, will not be able to accomplish this, because you will be resonating at much too high a frequency. Secondly, by not responding to the frequency accords of fear, distrust, and lies, you will be ensuring that the Planetary frequency continues to ascend. Ultimately, as enough people come to vibrate at these higher frequencies, the collective accord of love and light will swamp the slower frequencies, and ultimately transform them. The third and perhaps most important aspect, will be that the new frequencies will usher in a whole range of new vibrations that will replace and expand the awareness of all human beings on the Planet. The myth of enslavement by slower frequencies, encompassing worry, stress, fear, anger, and greed, will be replaced by a much greater harmony of heart and mind. This will allow the collective frequencies of unconditional love, and purity of intent and action, to underlie the fabric and basis of your lives. This is not some 'airy-fairy' promise. It will become a reality when over fifty percent of the slower frequencies on Earth have been removed.

The only predominant question that remains is the time-scale for all of this to take place. It is always extremely difficult to predict time-scales, because there are so many variables. However, suffice it to say that the more the twin frequencies of love and light are invoked and anchored into the Planet, by as many people as possible, then the more rapid will be this process. It is through your capacity to trust in this thought form — to believe that the thought forms of the Sixth Root Race will become reality — and through your ability to love, that this transformation will unfold. Once these features have been accepted, then the process will speed up rapidly.

So, when we speak of frequencies of the heart, we are indicating many different things: things that have to be felt, known by intuition, and acknowledged within the very depths of your being. The different, higher frequencies that have been referred to throughout this book are all important: they are all keying-in signatures for opening your heart, for building a bridge to your own inner divinity, and for exercising your will by calling in the highest frequencies of love and light. Connecting with the Paramatman and the Avataric Frequencies are the ultimate expression of this process. Nothing else matters.

The Heart as a Gateway

Once your heart has opened to these frequencies, then it is up to you how big you make the access point. Some people seem to think that if their heart centre can open a few inches, then they are doing pretty well. In reality, this is not terribly impressive, for it is possible for the space in your heart centre to expand way beyond the confines of your physical body; to encompass areas covering acres, miles, or even countries and continents. It is also possible for your heart centre to open a gateway into space, to connect with other planets, and to connect with, as we have seen, other frequencies and life-forms in different dimensions and on different planes. The choices are yours: in how much you trust and invoke, and in how far you are prepared to go to connect with the true potential, depth, and beauty of your heart centre.

As your heart centre begins to expand and resonate with the higher frequencies, as its aperture point expands, so you will experience, in rapid succession, a panoply of different love and light frequencies, each with its own brilliance and beauty. This is a part of the expansion, and it also indicates that the opening, and the accompanying clearing, are proceeding according to plan. These frequencies may take you unawares. They may connect at night, or while you are doing mundane tasks during the day. The key will be to trust the love flowing into your space, to accept this love as a gift, and to acknowledge the depth of connection between your heart and what is taking place. It will then be accurately said that you are operating from the heart rather than the head.

While previous Root Races have very much focused on the individual ascent into the Light, the Sixth Root Race is firmly locked into the collective ascent of all living creatures. This is an unprecedented opportunity for all to participate; to connect and to commune with the Divine in this extraordinary experiment of love and light.

Rays of Light

One informational aspect that has not yet been touched upon concerns the different ray types of light. There are many detailed explanations of the ray types, although perhaps the most comprehensive are those found in the writings of Alice Bailey and the Tibetan Djwhal Khul[2]. All of us have incarnated on a different light stream[3]. Each stream of light represents a different ray type, and each has a series of different qualities associated with it. Each ray type is expressed, at its most pure and fundamental, within the heart centres of every living being, although ray types are at their most evolved within the human form. Each one, while conveying its own frequency-vibration, will also have, as its subtler aspects, different combinations of other ray types, which are expressions of past life connections. So for example, a person's primary colour or light expression may be purple, which will reveal or unfold a series of qualities associated with, or integral to, that light stream. By the same token, the secondary light rays will also express or integrate various qualities, although to a lesser degree than the primary colours.

> As each heart centre begins to open as a result of the invitations sent out by the Spiritual Hierarchy to connect with the new frequencies, the fundamental ray types or colour types within each person will begin to resonate more deeply and exquisitely. It will be as if the qualities expressed within each ray type will be amplified and intensified. Consequently, the purples, pinks, golds, blues, greens, reds, and so on, will be expressed in a more vibrant way within the physical, etheric, and astral structures of each individual. Of course, this primary seeding of the new vibrations will emanate at first from the mental planes, but the physical expression of the anchoring of the different light frequencies into the Planet will be of major significance. The qualities associated with each of these light streams will become clearer, and the potential for greater blending of them will also present itself.

Blending Light Streams

> Blending of light streams will arise within each individual, and between individuals. What is especially valuable is the collective blending of these different ray types. There are seven basic ray types, and as each of these harmonises and blends within different collectives of expression (groups), the resultant impact on

people's heart centres will be seen in that they will vibrate more strongly, and will be able to hold the higher frequencies more adeptly and forcefully, as the waves of light enter their system. Put simply, these light frequencies will act as primary anchor points around the Planet for introducing the expanded ray types into the etheric and physical vehicles of all living creatures.

The expanded awareness and consciousness of the Sixth Root Race will provide a unique opportunity for all of you to connect more deeply with your fundamental ray type, and, through merging and mixing with other people, to access the frequency-vibrations of those operating from a different ray type. The physical and empathetic reaction that each of you will feel during this process will help you to gauge the significance of each ray type for you. For some, there will not be many gaps in their experiences in this respect. For others, there will be more gaps. The degree of blending, and the need to connect with various primary rays, will be an extremely profound experience for all of you. It will help to cement the basis for a truly collective association which has, as its hallmark, the greatest diversity and depth of light frequencies, ray types, and primary and secondary blending of ray types.

Primary and Secondary Colours

One result of this blending, coupled with a deeper understanding of the ray types, will be the ability to access the varying connections that you have with each of the primary and secondary colours. An easy way to do this is to fill your body, from head to toe, with a different colour. The choice of colour is entirely up to you; it can be selected intuitively, and you can work at varying its hue and tone. With each colour you try, you will feel a different-frequency vibration, a different emphasis within your physical and subtle bodies, and a difference in resonance with each of your chakras, depending upon the colour selected. You should find that some colours more than others will feel comfortable within your space — most especially within your heart centre — and this simple experiment will give you guidelines along which to sense your dominant colour connections, and to work with them. In time, you will learn to strip away the superficial associations that you may, through physical experience, have assigned to those colours, and with practice you will begin to register their inner potency, and the meaning that this has for you.

This stage of the process is particularly meaningful because it is initiating an outward expansion of your expression, and an inner linking with your deeper self. The resonant purity of vibration (or quality of feeling) within your chosen frequencies will then guide you to a deep recognition of your principal ray type or colour frequency. Subsequent working with this frequency-vibration within your heart will allow you to access your deeper connections more rapidly.

Although these suggestions and guidelines are extremely simple, they are also very powerful. The light frequencies that you select, and place in your heart, can serve as the building blocks for your interpretation of the new frequencies that can enter your heart, and which can then be built upon through trust, dedication and love. Each colour is an expression of the Divine, and each will provide you with access to a much deeper level within your whole being.

The Ray Types

While it is beneficial to work with the colours on an intuitive level, it is also helpful to have a background intellectual understanding of their qualities and attributes, and of their associated ray types. The ray types, as set out by Djwhal Khul[4], can be summarised as follows:

1. The Ray of Will, or Power
2. The Ray of Love-Wisdom
3. The Ray of Activity or Adaptability
4. The Ray of Harmony, Beauty, Art, or Unity
5. The Ray of Concrete Knowledge or Science
6. The Ray of Abstract Idealism or Devotion
7. The Ray of Ceremonial Magic, or Law

Each of these rays has its own set of characteristics, and each is linked to a specific spectrum of colour. As your heart opens up, it may be of interest for you to place this opening process within the context of your given ray type. It is not the purpose of this discussion to enable you to do this comprehensively, but rather to allow you to feel the many ways in which you can come to understand yourself on a deeper level.

> Anything that is placed in your heart, and which resonates there in peace and tranquillity, is showing you a part of your heart; a special frequency of your heart. This is the place where you can discover the true nature of love — its peacefulness, its silence, and serenity — and apply those attributes to your everyday life. This then becomes what some may call 'living in the moment', but in truth, it is much more than this. It is living in the heart, by the heart, of the heart, and for the heart. There can be no greater proof of the achievement of 'being centered'.

Hallmarks of the Heart

> What is sometimes difficult for people to accept is that all of these changes happen *within* them. They are not easily seen by those around you — not that this matters. What does matter is that the heart, in its infinite path of expansion, should begin to feel the true hallmarks of its own divinity, the hallmarks of its unfolding. This is more difficult, and indeed is beset by expectations and fears.

Once you have tasted the truth in your heart, nothing that you have known and enjoyed before is so relevant, so enticing, or so important to you. The unfurling of your heart, and its opening to the new frequencies, is showing you the way home. However, what happens to many during this process, is that the heart connection comes and goes: one minute it is there, and you are enraptured by its intensity, its beauty and, in some cases, the true bliss of it, and then suddenly it is gone. For many, this is a frightening experience, but this resonant opening and closing, much like that of the petals of a flower during day and night, is actually a hallmark of the heart. At first, it is always difficult to maintain the frequency-rapport for any length of time, so the depth of the heart connection, and consequently your connection with the love and light, will come and go. This is to be expected. It is important not to despair, but to realise that with trust and love, the connection will become more consistent. The slow trickle will become faster, and will then become a small stream, and so on, until, ultimately, the heart and its connection to the Divine will be as a roaring river leading into the Divine Ocean of Oneness.

Apart from temporary losses of connection, there are other hallmarks of the heart which can ensnare the unwary, many of them a result of the ego's battle to reassert its dominance over the heart. They can include a sense of unworthiness, or the converse — an arrogance which believes that there is nothing more to learn, and also delusions of grandeur. These are all traps of the mind, which need to be examined in the light of one's heart connection. A willingness to allow the heart to seek out and express our deeper fears, insecurities, and concerns, is another important hallmark. The compassion that we bring to bear, from our heart, will help to guide us through the maze of the mind. However seemingly insurmountable the problem or the emotional turmoil, trusting in the heart, and allowing the love to flow through it, will always assist us to connect with our deeper levels. Let us allow the input of higher frequencies of love and light to burn away the residue of old fears and insecurities.

> Perhaps the most important hallmark of the heart is the emergence of a sense of compassion for yourself, and for those around you. This will form the bedrock from which you can expand your heart connection, and feel your way into your true nature. For the Divine Father is known as the Compassionate Father, and it is this connection which will grow and grow within you, until it *becomes* you. This compassionate love from the Divine Father is one of the greatest gifts that can be given to others. You have only to look around today to realise that it still remains an extremely rare commodity. This, fortunately, will change.
>
> There are other hallmarks of the heart that will emerge as you progress. These will become emblazoned on your heart as it begins to resonate with the Sixth Root Race vibration. Ultimately, the true hallmark of the heart will be a recognition of your own divinity, and a connection with the Divine Father and Divine Mother which will remain forever imprinted in your heart.

Quantum Connections of the Heart

> As has already been indicated, the capacity for compassionate understanding and love is a key aspect of the heart. The stepping-down of Avataric and other frequencies through the heart centre is critical at this time, and will act as a sign-post for future heart connections. As we have also seen, there are many links that can be formed with different frequencies through the heart, and it is about these that we wish to say a little more.
>
> Earlier, we discussed the notion of quantum connections, and how new and more vibrant connections can be established within your space, due to the increasing frequency-vibrations

entering the Planet. The same is fundamentally true of the heart. The significant raising of heart vibration can be likened to quantum jumps of expression. The shift from the expression of love in a conditional way, to the expression of a much purer kind of love is something to behold. The soul's recognition, and the subsequent recognition by the personality, that ever deeper streams of the love vibration can be accessed, is indeed momentous.

What do we mean by this? Well, the shift, or quantum shift, is seen as a major change in vibration and frequency expansion within the heart. When this occurs, the older notions of what love means are replaced by a more profound perception: it becomes an experience of pure reality. In following the steps up the 'ladder' of love vibrations, each step, if you like, signifies a major rise in frequency and level of understanding. For example, you will begin to understand your connections with those around you, and with those people with whom you have interacted in the past. It will become clearer that many of your deeper love bonds are with those who may, on the face of things, give you a difficult time, or put you through the emotional 'mill', as it were. This can only be achieved, in many instances, by the love that person has for you *on the inner planes*. On the physical plane, he or she may be giving you a difficult time, or emotionally 'tickling' you, or providing a point of significant pressure for your personality. To understand at a deeper level the interplay of karma, the depth of commitment between you, can often help put a problem into perspective. Seeing a 'difficult' situation in a more balanced light, as a learning opportunity, represents a quantum shift in your heart. This is but one end of the scale.

Other aspects of the quantum heart-shift can be felt when the love that is expressed between two people evolves towards a more unconditional state, where there is no need for either partner to hide behind an aspect of themselves, or to project aspects of themselves on to each other. This true opening of the heart is felt as a particular vibration within the heart. Sometimes this opening is accompanied by a physical sensation, such as a deep pain, or a deepening of feeling in the heart.

These deeper interplays and expressions can then be expanded to include the love of a Divine Being, and the deeper connection that is felt in such interactions. In all cases, as the frequency is progressively stepped up, so the heart can respond in leaps and bounds. 'Quantum leaps of the heart' is one way in which the progressive opening of your heart can be described. No doubt you will find other ways to describe it.

As the Divine interplay of love and light is expressed within your heart centre, and spreads to the rest of your physical vehicle, so it is that the quantum connections can be built up. The heart centre acts as the primary portal for these interactions, but other centres can interact, and can resonate empathetically with it. When the other centres vibrate in unison with the heart centre, then a true balance of love and light can be found within the physical vehicle, and in its connections with the various subtler bodies. This is a rare and profoundly beautiful achievement.

Transformation Through the Heart

The quantum connections expressed through the twin frequencies of light and love will have a number of important ramifications. The light frequencies that are seeded into the heart centres of humanity will change the outlook and perspective of what is, and what is not acceptable. The strength and depth of these feelings will be felt clearly, and will allow the older practices to be swept away by the tidal wave of new frequencies. The heart must go before all, and everything must be connected to the heart vibration. If a particular object, a particular action, a particular thought, serves to move you away from your heart connection rather than towards it, it should be dropped, and offered up to the light for Divine transformation. This will build and build, so that every single facet of your life can be scrutinised in this way.

Although this may sound overwhelming at first, it should not be, because the unfolding of this process of scrutiny will happen step-by-step. There will be no sudden shifts that you will be unable to cope with; it will become clear, as part of a natural process, that certain activities move you away from your heart, while others bring you closer. You will find that the former make you feel less connected and less happy, and the latter make you feel a deeper love connection. It will be obvious which you prefer, and which gives you more vitality and integrity. Trust in this.

So the heart will come to represent your core, your truth, and the yard-stick by which to measure your life. All will flow naturally, and all will be expressed through the love and light that are now entering the Planet so ferociously. You will discover that there are numberless frequencies of the heart. Explore them, connect with them, and feel the depth of the love that you hold within you. You will amaze yourself — you may not have thought these things possible. But as you do connect, you will come to realise that the transformations that we have been talking about, in terms of the Sixth Root Race, are *all* possible, and that they *will* become a reality. They will come about despite the reservations and fears that you hold inside of yourself at this time. They will come about because the higher aspects of yourself, the higher dictates of your heart, all demand that they should. All you need do is go with the flow of your heart, and find that at the end of the journey, your true divinity and birthright will become one with you.

Your heart will resonate with love, joy, and a sense of calm and tranquil unity with all around you, on every level. This is the dream that is promised; this is the vision that is being ushered in, from the inner and outer planes. Connect and commune with your own divinity, and realise that the true Divine is but a step away, a thought away, and that **it has been within you all along.** Reclaim it and recall it through the opening and expansion of your true heart. These are truly keys to your heart.

The Divine Heart

The frequencies that are an expression of the Divine Heart are a culmination and an amalgam of all the possible heart vibrations present on your Planet, and many more besides. They defy definition. They are beyond anything that you imagine. They are the sum total of the God-Head[5] and are a reflection of all the true Divinity within the Universe and beyond. In seeking to align yourself with the Divine Heart, while you cannot achieve a total merging, and will not achieve a total merging until God-realisation, you can, as it were, sample some of the Divine Frequencies by seeking an alignment of intent and love. This much can be given.

For in truth, a complete alignment would transcend all that is present in duality in your world, and would uncover the True Divine, and the limitless Ocean of Love and Light. So to aspire to connect with the Divine Heart, with the manifested expression of such love, is the beacon guiding you home. We salute you, and acknowledge your path to the Divine Heart.

Connect in love, with integrity, and without expectation. The true love and divinity that will be experienced will be beyond description, beyond thoughts, and, in one sense, beyond feelings, since this would suggest a possible division between you and the Divine. You will sense a glimpse of the Union, the Divinity, and the all-encompassing Oneness of Divine Bliss. You may hold this frequency for only a short time — a few seconds, a few minutes. It does not matter. This experience will provide you with your beacon, your homing signal, and that which you need to aspire to in the future.

The Christos and Crystalline Frequencies

The expression of Divine love, as it is emerging through the Sixth Root Race frequency, is a stepping-stone to this new attunement and attainment. Many centuries into the future, what will be made manifest will surely be an expression of the Seventh Root Race, which will build on the excellence of the Sixth, and further express the Divine Plan. For now, though, the expression of Divine Love, of pure Light, of the Paramatman Light, into the Sixth Root Race, will set such a high level of crystalline energy and love, that it will set a new standard of connection and attunement to the Divine Heart. This is the promise, or rather a facet of the promise, that was made during the time of the Christ or the Christos[6]. The resonance of the Christos with the Sixth Root Race is no accident. Many have predicted the return of the Christ in physical form, in what may be termed the Second Coming, but the sense in which this is expressed is misinterpreted: it does not do justice to the key promise which is that the Christos energies will return as an expression of the pure Divinity of the Sixth Root Race, for the simple reason that They will form one of the central foundation stones of the emergence of the Sixth Root Race crystalline frequency.

So, in the Sixth Root Race, one of the more profound frequencies that will be explored will be the crystalline frequencies derived from the Christos. They will also be seeded by other Divine Aspects, which will become clearer with time. Just as the Sixth Root Race is a culmination of all that has gone before, in terms of frequencies, both light and dark, so it is that the Avataric Presences which have graced the Planet in ages past will be re-seeded within Sixth Root Race consciousness. The alignments of these frequencies will then present a key for opening the Divine Logos[7], and will allow a stepping-up of all humanity to connect with the Divine Heart in a more powerful manner. This is where the true and ultimate keys to your heart will be found.

The resonant heart-beat or pulse that will accompany the alignment of the Sixth Root Race thought form with the Divine Heart will send out an octave of energy that will spread across millions of frequencies, and millions of soul aspects incarnated on the Planet at this time.

Liquid Light of Crystalline Love

The Divine Heart will embody, in the Sixth Root Race, the liquid light of crystalline love. This harmonising and unifying pulse beat will sound an accord through all the heart centres of light workers, and of others who are called to the Sixth Root Race attunement. This frequency rapport will stream into all of your hearts, opening within you a gateway which will allow the ascension of your heart centre into an alignment with the Divine Heart. The octave that will envelop you can be likened to a liquid light of crystalline love, reaching through time and space to a place within you which will be the resonant beacon for your true home-coming. This will be the dominant frequency octave which will call to all of you and which will sing in your heart. Your heart will reverberate with true divinity, purity, peace, and tranquillity.

This crystalline rapport will open the gates of your heart, one by one, through each ascending level, until ultimately your heart-beat has total attunement with the planetary heart-beat, the Divine Heart-beat, and the heart-beat of the Sixth Root Race. This will be true attunement, true alignment, and true resonance.

So, as your heart receives the call of Divine Love, the Divine Message to connect more deeply with the Divine Heart, run towards your true destiny within the frequency dance of the Sixth Root Race accord. This call to the heart will be unlike any other calling. It is the only true call from the Divine Father Meher Baba.

The opening of the individual heart to embrace the Divine Heart in as many ways as possible, lies at the core of the Sixth Root Race. The key to your heart is truly the Divine Heart, the Divine Heart which unifies and is One with the Divine Ocean of Love, expressing in Oneness the Divine Father's Fire and the Divine Mother's Love. Reach out and ask for It. Call upon It at all times, in all situations, and feel the soothing tranquillity and the liquid light of pure crystalline love flowing into your very being. Feel the ever-deepening unification of your physical self, with your higher self, with your soul, and ultimately with the Divine Ocean of Love. Feel this connection always. Once connected, always in communication and in communion.

Chapter 7 • Divine Healing of the Heart

The frequency-vibrations that are now entering your heart space have been accorded the highest frequencies levels at this time. This is not to say that you will not connect with slower frequencies within your heart space as you move more deeply into the clearing and cleansing process, but rather that the blueprint for your heart's development is being mapped out as we speak; and the core message is that the Divine Love of the Father will heal your heart. Many of you may feel that your hearts do not need healing, but there is always a place for healing, and it will arise as part of your jouney to the Divine Flame of inspiration. What has now been set in motion within your heart space is nothing short of miraculous.

We spoke earlier in this book of some of the processes of clearing and cleansing your inner space, and of removing the old seeds of mischief and distrust. Probably the most important location for this process is your heart. Over the many thousands of lives that you have been through, you will have experienced numerous openings of the heart to admit the Divine Frequencies of love and light, but at other times, in other lives, slower, darker frequencies have closed off your heart from the Father's Love. This too, is an essential part of the process. However, throughout this journey, as you have moved onwards and upwards towards the unification of your soul with that of the over-soul[1] and ultimately with God the Divine, the space within your heart, on all levels, has been expanding. It has also been excising the conflicts of the past — the heart centre is somewhat akin to a 'cauldron' of old frequencies, some beautiful, some not so beautiful.

Clearing the Heart

This cauldron of frequencies, this panoply of experiences of the heart, is now reaching a turning point, a point of no return, within the Divine Plan on Earth. The frequencies now entering the Planet, and the vibration of love and light inherent within them, provide a unique opportunity for offering up all older frequencies to the Divine Father and Divine Mother. This is part of the ending of the old contracts, and the ushering-in of the new ones. In short, the new frequencies offer the potential for unlimited healing of your heart, and ultimately a deep Divine Healing for your soul.

What do we mean by 'older' frequencies? Well, for many people, one simple but profound way of looking at it is as follows. Imagine, if you can, all of the times when you have been in battles, or other situations involving death and bloodshed. If you symbolise each of these experiences as a sword, then you may feel within your heart centre a whole host of swords. In fact, there will be bundles and bundles of them, each representing the older frequency accords of war and bloodshed, whether performed by you, or inflicted on you. These older frequencies, these older bundles, will be offered up to the light, offered up to the Divine, as part of the accord of cleansing and clearing. This removal from your heart centre of the swords of despair and distrust, pain and anguish, will represent the first phase in what can be called 'Divine Healing of the Heart'.

Highways of the Heart

The second phase of Divine Healing will build rapidly on the first. The space that will have been cleared within your heart, will allow a bridge to be built within its centre, leading to the inner planes, and upwards through the etheric and astral levels to the mental planes. The beauty of this bridge will initiate a new-frequency rapport between your physical vehicle, your higher-self in its many different aspects, and the binding of your soul to the collective and Divine Will of the Father. It will be unlike any other bridge, for it will grow and expand as your heart grows and expands. It will allow a two-way path of higher heart frequencies to travel the timelines of your heart, timelines which will begin to unravel all that is for you in the past, present, and future. The true bridge to self-realisation, and ultimately to God-realisation, can only be built with the highest frequencies of love and light: those frequencies which are encompassed in their entirety by the Paramatman Light.

As these frequencies ascend, and as the bridge of love is strengthened and broadened into a highway of your divinity, so it is that the segregation of frequencies will come about. This was mentioned earlier, and it represents a segregation of the old from the new. The older frequencies of the Fifth Root Race will drop away, and will be replaced by the Sixth Root Race galactic highway of love and pure intent. The segregation will manifest itself in many different ways, but perhaps one of the most forceful will be the way in which the older, slower frequencies of distrust, hatred, violence, destruction, and fear will simply drop away. It will not be possible, by virtue of the frequency resonance or vibration of your heart centre, for these old frequencies to slow you, or to drag your vibration down again. So where in the past you will have felt fear and worry, these will be replaced by the highest frequencies of love and light: the older frequencies will thus no longer hold sway.

This may seem difficult to visualise at present, given all the pain, death, and destruction occurring around the Planet. Nevertheless it will happen. There are small pockets of love and perfection, such as the places where the Avatar has lived His physical life. There are places of rare beauty and exquisite perfection on the Planet. Find them and anchor your vibration into them. They will multiply, and will call forth more resonances with other sites. For this exercise you need to use your heart and your intuition. Your heart will tell you what you feel; it will tell your truth, for you alone, regarding any given place. Your heart is anchored into the Divine Love and Light emanating from the mental planes, and your heart attunes you to your surroundings. This is what is meant by the expression 'home is where the heart is'. In this way, wherever you go, whoever you are with, you will be at home, because you will be anchored in your heart, and anchored in the full certainty and knowledge of the Divine Love that is freely flowing up and down your 'highway of the heart'. This represents the second phase of 'Divine Healing of the Heart'.

Collective Superhighways of the Heart

The third phase represents and requires the introduction of the collective intent of the group heart. This is not as straightforward as it may sound: it is not a pooling of all light workers who have connected with the Divine through their own 'highway of the heart'. It is much, much more than this. For each individual who has established within his or her heart centre a resonant frequency bridge to the inner planes, to the higher mental planes (what we have called a 'highway of the heart'), there will be a *collective* counterpart that is demanded of each group setting that is established. One of the key aspects of the Sixth Root Race is working in the collective, in the group, the collective frequency rapports that can be sustained by group living, by group harmonisation, being much greater than those sustained through the individual. Just as each individual can build a bridge from his or her heart centre to the inner planes, so it is that each group can build a collective bridge of Divine Intent to the inner planes. We say again: this is not just a combination of the respective 'highways of the heart' of each group member.

What is being invoked is a *group* bridge, a *collective* bridge, which will resonate on all the frequencies of the individual components of the group, and will also bridge any gaps in their frequencies. As these frequencies harmonise and blend, the process can be likened to the weaving of a tapestry which will contain within it a vast array of frequencies, experiences, soul connections, past life connections, and above all, a diversity of paths to the Divine. It is said that there as many ways to God as there are people. This is indeed true, and the frequency bridges that are meshed together within a group setting can establish, if you like, a superhighway to the mental planes, a bridge to the higher Divine Frequencies. These Divine Frequencies are such that they can rarely be accessed by individuals, but through group intent, group love, and the construction of the super-highway of love within the group space of all the individuals involved, it will be possible to build a group heart of Divine Intent. This group heart is consolidated, and connected to the Divine Father and Divine Mother by all those who call upon these twin aspects of Divinity.

So just as each of us has within him, a highway of the heart, so it is that the group can build and cement a superhighway that is aligned with the highest frequencies of Divine Love and the Paramatman Light. The group can anchor these frequencies into the Planet, and the group heart can then become, as it were, a mini-chakra within the Planetary frequencies. The establishment of these group chakras, these mini-chakras of the Planet, will have enormous catalytic potential in the opening of the hearts and minds of all those around. From small acorns grow large oaks, and so it is that with the collective intent of the group, the oaks of Divine Love can spring up throughout the Planet, ensuring the segregation of the new frequencies, and ensuring that the Divine Plan is ushered in.

Planet of the Heart

The fourth aspect or manifestation of 'Divine Healing of the Heart' can be best summarised as the 'Planet of the Heart'. Earth, as a planet of free will, has a unique combination of frequencies, and can be said to be a planet of the heart and head, the balance being fifty percent heart and fifty percent head. Up to now, the prevailing frequency of the planetary heart has been predominantly negative, so just as the hearts of all human beings require healing, so it is for the Planet. One of the seeding mechanisms for this healing is the creation of mini-chakras through group love and group intent. At the same time, the new frequencies called in by the Paramatman and by the Photon Belt will help to activate Earth's heart centre in a totally new and awe-inspiring way. The planetary heart centre was, until recently, India, but the new vibrations have shifted it to South Africa. This country of great beauty, which at present is a melting-pot of old and new frequencies, will be the scene for the transformation of Earth's heart chakra.

Again, just as the heart chakras of all light workers need to be cleared and cleansed, so it is with the Planetary heart chakra. All of the old frequencies of distrust, and of battles — of beliefs and of bodies — will need to be cleared. This is already happening, as can be seen in the dramatic shifts that have already taken place in South Africa. However, much more is needed there, and as the segregation of frequencies continues, the clearing of old burial sites, of old battle grounds, and old areas of despair and fear, must continue. The planetary heart-beat is taken from this area, and as the clearing continues, so the beat will quicken. The two will go hand-in-hand.

As the healing of South Africa continues and accelerates, the Divine Frequencies of love and light will be stepped-up into the Planet, which itself will undergo a transformation and segregation of frequencies, which will mirror what is happening to all living beings, both on and below its surface. Much of the planetary clearing which needs to take place within the astral and mental planes will be made possible by this opening of the heart chakra of the Planet. It will be as if a planetary highway of love and light will be formed between the Planet and its Divine counterparts on the inner planes. The elevated and exulted status of Earth as a 'finishing school' of old will be re-established. This, therefore, represents the fourth aspect of 'Divine Healing of the Heart'. It will arise as part of a deeper connection with, and reverence for, Earth by the many life-forms she supports, and in particular, through the transfer of the guardianship of your Planet back to the human race. The symbiotic relationship of the heart, from the individual person, to the group or collective dynamic, and ultimately to the Planetary heart, are all deeply and inextricably interconnected.

Further Aspects of Divine Healing of the Heart

While it is slightly premature to discuss the fifth and sixth aspects of 'Divine Healing of the Heart', it is worth noting that the fifth aspect will take on a more cosmic or galactic dimension. The highways of the heart, the super-highways of the group heart, and the planetary highway of the heart, will all merge to usher in a new, dimensional heart connection with other planets, other star systems, and our extra-terrestrial star-sisters and brothers. Once this has happened, the Divine Frequencies will spread far and wide. Initially, this will be through connections made with some of our older star-brothers and sisters, and those planets with which Earth has a karmic connection.

In those cases where the karmic connection has been of a more negative disposition, such as in those with Mars or Lyra, the potential for redressing the karmic balance will present itself. This is still some way off, though, and should not be expected within any of our lifetimes. In the remaining cases, i.e. those where the karmic interaction has resonated according to the higher dictates of love and light, the resonant harmonic frequencies of love and light which will be set up, or re-initiated, will call in a higher frequency accord. Our connection with Sirius is an example of this.

In the meantime, as these planetary karmic plays are enacted, the connections and harmonic resonant vibrations between the human race and its disparate extra-terrestrial ancestors and star-brothers and sisters, will begin to hold sway. These connections will begin to bring about a true alignment of the hearts and minds of all those concerned, whether it be on the inner planes or on the physical. The highways of the heart will surely bring about a Divine Play of love that will bring such great joy to all involved.

The sixth and final aspect of 'Divine Healing of the Heart' is the ultimate connection, and refers, in every aspect, to the Divine Union of the Soul with the Divine Ocean. This is the ultimate Union. It is the final healing, the final acknowledgement of true Divine Love, the final mir-roring between the Divine and the individual soul aspect. In a sense, the wheel has come full circle again, for in this aspect, it is the individual who becomes one with the Divine. However, the Sixth Root Race, through its emphasis on the group, on the collective, is initiating a shift in this aspect. It is a shift into a Divine Union between the *group* and the Divine Ocean, rather than the individual. So, the promise that has been made, and the promise that has been honoured, is one of collective real-isation and group union with the Divine.

> We have, therefore, described the different aspects of 'Divine Healing of the Heart'. The frequencies that you will ultimately recognise in this process will literally 'blow your mind', because they will give a signal which the mind will recognise as an ulti-mate truth — a truth to which the mind will be unable to respond in its normal fashion, and which will allow your very essence to connect with Divine Truth, Divine Love, and Divine Knowledge. As you sample the Divine connection, as you ascend the various steps of healing frequencies, as you connect ever

more deeply with your heart, you will come to recognise what your truth is, where your true connection lies, and the manner in which you can access it most directly. This is the promise accorded by the Sixth Root Race vibration.

Healing the Wounds of the Heart

There are other ways in which 'Divine Healing of the Heart' can have a dramatic impact. For many of you, what you perceive as deep pain in your heart, which may have been awakened through the unrequited love of old karmic ties, can provide you with valuable information about your own process, and the healing that is required. Many of you have felt deceived, used, and traumatized through an array of relationships which have, in a very real sense, left you wounded. These wounds may seem fresh, open, and all-too-recent, but in truth they represent, in many instances, very *old* wounds, which have been reactivated according to the new alignment of energies. If they were not reactivated or re-opened, then the older karmic and energetic charges associated with them would cause you much greater pain in the future, when these energies will have ascended to even higher octaves of love and light.

It is as if you have a wound which has been obscured by shadows for a very long time. When a light is first shone in the darkness it can be painful to the eyes. But imagine if this light was so bright and powerful that it would even be hard to acclimatise to it in normal daylight. Imagine how much harder this would then be if such a light were to blaze in the darkness. You would be totally overwhelmed. So it is with the emotional traumas that many of you are working through now. It is much better that these old wounds be first cleared of any old charges, and then cleansed, and finally allowed to heal in the current climate of energies, rather than at a future date when the energies are even more demanding than they are now.

So the planning and circumstances that have brought many of you to this point of disturbance, emotional trauma, and deep, heart-felt pain, have done so for a reason, which is to allow you to access these old wounds, and to initiate a deep clearing process. A similar process is happening all over the Planet: earth movements, floods, volcanoes, and oceanic tidal currents are throwing up old wounds that now have the chance to be cleansed and healed.

These processes are painful on one level, but deeply liberating on another, and as more space is created in your heart, so it is that more light and love can be accessed by it. This, then, reflects a truer sense of the term 'healing'.

The heart vibrations which are being stepped-up in tempo will, by virtue of their very resonance and strength, uncover and heal many of these old wounds, which you have been carrying over many lifetimes. This process is necessary for two reasons: firstly, the clearing is necessary in order to facilitate expansion and growth in your connection with the Divine. Secondly, the experiences that you gain during this clearing will enable you to support and connect with others who will go through similar experiences at a later date, as part of the succession of elevated frequencies. Consequently, your role in this process, as the first wave of participants, is as trail-blazers, if you like, and as teachers of those following behind in your footsteps. Remember this, for it will be most important in future years.

Divine Service

There is much more that can be considered in terms of 'Divine Healing of the Heart'. In earlier chapters we spoke of the Avataric Network, and Its multi-dimensional role in the Planet's evolution and in humankind's evolution into the Sixth Root Race. The Avataric Network will, of course, play a defining role in healing the hearts of millions of people, whether this be directly, or through their agents in matter. This means that there will be manifold opportunities for you to connect with the Divine Energies through invocation, through irradiation on many different levels, and through direct physical contact if you so choose. This latter course, while not strictly necessary, will certainly speed up the process of your heart's healing, so that you can be labelled a true 'heart worker', i.e. one who works directly through the heart in all its many facets. This will be your gift and your birthright, and will also position you to be of Divine service at all times and in all circumstances.

Healing Through the Heart into Death

Simply through the irradiation of frequencies in your heart, you will be bringing through the higher vibrations necessary for healing; and as you heal, so shall you be healed. The two processes will be 'arm-in-arm' as it were. As your connection deepens, the heart frequencies which you can house and handle will ascend continuously, and will allow many of the older, slower frequencies to clear automatically. This is all part of the process, part of the unfolding; and it is also part of the ritual of living and dying. The 'relationship' that you have with your own death will also be determined by the degrees to which your heart is healed, opened, and expanded. For in truth, since many of you have a morbid fear of death, it will become clearer that the only way to reconcile this issue is through trusting in your own divinity, and trusting in your heart, and what it has to tell you about this subject.

For while you may have experienced millions of deaths, it is always the most recent experiences which will determine your current attitude to it. For some of you, the need to open your awareness, and to trust in an existence beyond death, will require a 'near death experience'. Those who have already been confronted by such experiences recognise them as pivotal points in their life, offering, as they do, an expansion of the consciousness into a new, more dynamic connection with death. Living and dying are interconnected — some would say that they are two sides of the same coin. However, death provides an opportunity, an opening into another level of existence and experience. This experience is as real as this life which you currently perceive or experience, although the crossing-over from 'living' to the 'after-life' state may be a shock for some of you.

What has this to do with the heart, some of you may ask? Well, the love and the Divine Fire within you are all intertwined, whether you experience 'living' or 'dying'. The heart is what connects you to the Divine. It is the connection which transcends all others, so as your body dies, your heart connection with the Divine will remain as vibrant as ever, and will provide you with the means to connect with your higher-self, your soul, in the 'after-life' state. It will be your defining beacon as you transfer from the 'living' state into the 'after-life' experience.

This consideration of bringing our own death into our heart connection is an extremely important one. For death, and the fear of our own death, presents a major blockage for many people. Whether the physical side of the death process comes about through accident, illness, or simply at the agreed time, many people harbour a deep fear of it. At the same time, they may also believe that there is nothing after death, and in a nihilistic way this then determines their attitude to life — in that there is only one life, and that you have to make of it as much as possible. Yet this may not be everyone's response: there will be some who, when confronted by this nihilism[2], fall into a deep depression, from which there seems no escape. The riposte from many people is "what is the point?" "Why bother?" To persuade them of another perspective is difficult, and indeed often misplaced, for it is only through igniting the glowing embers of Divine Love within their hearts, that they will begin to gain some perspective on the process of dying and the reasons for it.

What is so important in this unfolding, is to realise, at a physical, *feeling* level, the connection that we have through our heart with the Divine Father and Mother. The fear, worry, and burden of 'living' will become transformed by recognising the immortality of our heart connection in the process of 'dying'.

> So: *feel* into your death, not with fear, but with your heart. *Feel* what this connection tells you. *Feel* what it has to offer you in understanding what your own death means. Sometimes the heart has to heal itself through dying, and through death itself. This is nothing to be afraid of. It is simply a process that connects you more and more deeply with your own divinity, and your own immortality.
>
> Therefore, death is not something to be afraid of. It is part of the heart's journey to God, it is part of the transition of states, from living to the after-life; and an understanding of this process will also bring you into a deeper connection with your heart. Whether you are 'alive' or in the after-life state, God will always be with you. This is part of the great adventure, the great experiment.

There are, of course, various helpful things that can be done at the time of death. Connecting with the Paramatman Light, connecting with the Avatars, and invoking a clear connection with your soul, are all techniques which will facilitate the transition. It is said that if you chant the name of Meher Baba repeatedly just before you die, then He will meet you in the after-life. This is indeed a rare and beautiful gift!

Divine Healing of the Mind Through the Heart

One of the most difficult areas confronting many people in the West is the balance between the heart and the mind. Although we have discussed aspects of the process of moving from the head to the heart, and by implication, from the mind to the heart, difficulties remain.

Although we have anchored ourselves into our heart, it is as if a component or residue of the mind, which at once seems impregnable, stubborn, and immovable in its entirety, remains. Part of the solution to the problem lies in recognising that this aspect of mind, which appears so stubborn, is in fact an integral part of our evolution towards the One True Connection with the Divine.

The mind, even in a state of heart-felt connection, can continue to feel as if, at times, it has the upper hand, so having arrived at a deeper connection within our heart, there remains an all-too-obvious residue of the mind that cannot be shifted. It is at this point that we might choose to recognise that we have hit upon an aspect of the true nature of mind, i.e. that it refuses to let go; refuses to loosen its grip in describing and encompassing reality according to its own dictate, rather than heeding the soft calling of our heart.

> This aspect of mind, which has been with you throughout all your lifetimes in human incarnation, is but a direct reflection of your sanskaras, your deep karmic ties and patterns. Consequently, to attempt to control this aspect of mind into submission is futile. It will only lead to more mirrors for the mind to hide behind and reflect. Nor will pretending to ignore the mind, as if it was not there, provide you with a long-term answer: in seeking to ignore it, you are burying it beyond sight — but not beyond your reality. It will remain with you, and will contrive, at some later time, to break through the shackles of mindful ignorance, and to repossess your waking thoughts.
>
> No. The key question to be addressed is this: given that you have travelled such a distance within yourself to connect with your heart, is it perhaps no accident that the mind seeks to control your attention once more? Why is this? It should be clear that the process of connecting with your own divinity, and ultimately proceeding to a closer connection with the Divine Itself, has brought you to a place much closer to home, if not to the

doors of your true home. To be persuaded by the mind that somehow, having come this far, you need to change your approach, and your connection with the Divine is, of itself, and in itself, a complete illusion. This illusion, created by the mind, is that the ongoing *presence* of the mind, even when you have developed a strong, deep, vibrant heart connection, somehow shows the futility of your approach.

Nothing could be further from the truth, or from the dictates of your heart. The heart knows what is real and what is not real. The heart knows what is true for you and what is not true for you. And the heart knows, in its own silence, in its own peace, that the connection with the Divine is heartfelt, vibrant and powerful. None of this can the mind give you; none of this can the mind access. For all of this is beyond the mind.

So when you feel that somehow your mind is in control despite the increasing connection between your heart and the Divine, then at those times affirm that you do indeed have a vibrant connection with the Divine. Indeed, it is at this juncture that you need to invoke the Divine connection all the more powerfully, all the more deeply, for It will show you, beyond a shadow of a doubt, that the games of the mind are really no more than that: games. And that the ongoing stripping of sanskaras, the continued loosening of the vice-like grip of your mind upon your consciousness, can only really be brought about by the Divine, by the Divine Father, or Divine Mother.

During these times of difficulty, be sure to reconnect with the Divine Heart through your own heart; be sure to feel the flow of Divine Love within your space. For as you heal your heart, so shall you, in this, heal your mind. And despite what the mind may tell you, this can only be done through the Divine Heart.

This, in essence, is what 'Divine Healing of the Heart' is all about: the simple and clear truth that all you need to do is to connect to the Divine through your heart. This will provide you with all the resources that you need in your spiritual quest for Divine Unity. It will provide you with love, with trust, with compassion, with strength, with resolve, with perspective, with unity, and with consideration for all that is around you. In short, connecting with the Divine will automatically heal your heart; it will automatically take you closer to your home; it will automatically heal your mind; and it will forcibly remove the old sanskaric patterns which seek to hold you back on so many levels. Above all, it will provide you with Divine Love, and with the realisation that you can ask for more and more; that the supply is limitless, and never-ending. All you need to do is to ask.

So recognise at all times that you have the capacity, the right, and the intent to invoke the Divine Healing, the Divine Compassion, and the Divine Love. It is yours to access and receive in whatever way is appropriate for you.

Chapter 8 • Stellar Frequencies of the Heart

Stellar Heart Centres

The frequencies that fall within the planetary expression of your extra-terrestrial brothers and sisters also have much to teach you concerning heart vibrations, which is why it is appropriate to turn to this question of stellar frequencies of the heart. It is clear to many of you that the star known to you as the Sun, which acts as your main source of physical-plane light, also acts as a gateway to the heart of the Universe — to the heart of the Cosmos, if you like. Your scientists have hypothesised as to how stars have formed out of the "Big Bang"; how each individual star forms out of an agglomeration of inter-stellar gases; and how, once this mass of gases has reached a critical point, a new star or sun is born. This stellar evolution, like all things in the Universe, is held together by an invisible fabric, an invisible web: the web of light and love. Since stars are the principal sources of physical light within your universe, it is appropriate to refer to them as stellar heart centres; as centres of the heart which promote life, which foster planetary evolution, and which ultimately sacrifice their own evolution to the higher focus of universal evolution.

The frequencies represented by your Sun are magnificent. Indeed, they are beyond description and experience for you, although the Sun represents the heart centre of your solar system. It provides the light, the nourishment, and the harmonisation of all the ray types within the planetary planes. It manifests these ray types throughout all the spectrums of light, from infrared to ultra-violet, and way beyond that.

The Photon Belt

Now, the portals of light and love which your Sun represents, are closely connected with the greater expression and impact of the photon energy entering the solar system from the Photon Belt. Although the Photon Belt represents an extremely large region of space, which houses high-frequency photon energy, it is only through the *solar* connection that this photon energy is actually anchored into the Planet. In a sense, the Sun is providing a background matrix of frequencies that both enhance, and are enhanced by, the Photon Belt.

As the Planet continues its passage through the Photon Belt in the coming years, the frequency signals being emitted by the Sun will continue to build. While many of you have observed that the loss of the ozone layer is contributing to the increasing ferocity of the Sun, this ferocity is also due to the Photon Belt and its interaction with the solar frequencies. This effect will continue to build over the next twenty-five to thirty years. As the Photon Belt raises the frequency vibration of the Sun, so the Sun will raise the frequency vibration of the Planet. It will be, on one level, as if you are being 'energetically fried'.

The impact of these powerful solar frequencies on human and all other life-forms on the Planet will be momentous. They will have their main effect on the heart centres of all living beings, in that they will help to activate new frequency vibrations within them. For human beings, this will mean a further stepping-up of the planetary heart-beat, and the ascendancy of the heart vibration. The effect of this will be to forge a link between your own heart centre and the Sun itself. This idea may seem strange to you, but it becomes simpler if you realise that you already have a deep connection to the Sun, going back through aeons of time. Ancient civilisations that worshipped the Sun did so through design, not accident: they recognised the connection between the frequency vibrations within their heart and solar plexus, and those of the Sun.

The Solar Logos

The problem today is to reconnect the heart centre of all life-forms with the Sun, and to do it in a more dynamic and direct way. This will allow the expression of what is termed the Solar Logos[1] to begin to come through, and to be reflected within the emergence of the new Root Race of humankind. The Solar Logos represents a manifestation of the Solar Intent, or Solar Evolution, of your solar system. This is a concept that deserves to be explored in more detail.

By 'Logos' is meant, in traditional parlance, 'the Word': the Word of God. Since God is manifested in all things, and since all things, both physical and non-physical, are an expression of His Will, His Divine Intent, then the expression of His Will through the Sun is an expression of His Divine Fire, or His Divine Authority in matter. To speak of the Solar Fire, the Solar Logos, is to speak of change, in terms of the breakdown or destruction of the old in the Divine Fire, and also of the emergence of the new, which has been annealed in the Solar Fire. The Solar Logos, therefore, symbolises, on one level, an expression of Divine Fire: change on a grand scale initiated by the Father's Will, and the manifest expression of His Love through the purification in fire of the heart and mind.

This perhaps sounds a little daunting or 'over the top' as some may say. However, the energy within these words needs to be considered very carefully. The transformation of the individual, collective, and super-collective heart centre of the Sixth Root Race represents a massive purification, a mighty opening, and above all, an infusion of a host of new, emergent frequencies. This will lead to an ascension of all the heart vibrations to embody a new concept and experience of divinity, and of connection with the Divine. In a sense, the Solar Logos is a key aspect of Divine Intent; one which gives, through Fire, the authority and power for this transformation to come about.

Perhaps now the connection with the Sun and the heart centre is becoming clearer to you. It is the fiery aspect of Divine Love, of Divine Will, which is being expressed through the Solar Logos, and through a forging of a physical and non-physical link between the Sun, the Photon Belt, and the ascending frequencies of your hearts. No single aspect can fully operate in the absence of the other. No true kindling of the Divine Fire can occur without the input of photon energy.

The Divine Fire and Divine Purification

In the past, when the Sun was worshipped, the ritual was in many circumstances intended to embody an expression of solar purification. The fact that some of these practices had substantial sacrificial components can tend to distort the meaning of Divine Fire and Divine Purification. In its highest form, Divine Purification is purification of the soul. It is the embodiment of cleansing, on a soul level, of the impurities or experiences within. These purifications are directed at the sanskaras built up over numerous lifetimes, and this is the true sense of Divine Purification, since no other type of purification really has any significance except in the context of clearing one's sanskaras.

So the emergence of the Sixth Root Race will be accompanied by this Divine Purification, this cleansing of sanskaras, which will help one and all to connect ever more closely with God, through the Divine Fire: and this is one aspect of Its role.

Few people have considered the full implications of the Divine Fire and Its importance in the cleansing process, from the deepest levels to the physical plane level. In terms of the Sixth Root Race, the Divine Fire will flush out, individually and collectively, any sanskaras which would block the higher frequencies from entering our space. The combined effects of the Photon Belt, the invocation of light and love, and the inner and outer guidance supplied by the Spiritual Hierarchy, and in particular by the Avataric Network, will provide a platform for this cleansing process, which will work on the individual and collective levels, and also on the planetary level and beyond.

So, as the Divine Fire floods into your space, fills your mind and heart, and provides the necessary input of love and light to bring the sanskaric transformation to a point of significant karmic intensity, so it is that the bonds and ties of old will be released. One of the oldest aspects of this bondage concerns the slower-frequency patterns that have been repeatedly used on Planet Earth by some of the less friendly extra-terrestrial brothers. Indeed, the sanskaric ties between these extra-terrestrials and many of you, forms a foundation for your current dislike — or even fear — of extra-terrestrials.

The time has come for this bondage of old to be severed and transformed in the Divine Fire. Indeed, as your frequencies ascend and amplify, it will be extremely difficult for these old extra-terrestrial connections to hold sway with your etheric, astral, and physical patterns in the way that they used to. This will not be represented as a battle on the physical planes. Rather, it will arise as an inner-planes battle, as these older extra-terrestrials seek to re-access your system through the astral levels, and to play out the slower-frequency karmic dance which has been their hallmark through the ages.

Renegade DNA and the Living Library

Indeed, the destruction and havoc that have been inflicted on your subtle DNA structure, and its impact on the physical DNA structure, have caused you significant problems in realigning yourselves. They have also prevented you from establishing a high enough frequency-band for you to resonate with your older colleagues, who wish your growth and self-reliance to blossom. The slower-frequency, extra-terrestrial connections have, in the past, focused on segregating and mixing your renegade DNA through unfortunate ritualistic practices. These now need to be discarded. Your DNA vibration needs to ascend dramatically. It also needs to reintegrate those high-frequency renegade aspects which have been the focal point of all Root Race evolution, and Planetary stewardship. These older renegade frequencies also provide the keys to what is known as the 'Living Library'[2] of frequency intent, through the combined aspects of Divine Light and Divine Love.

The use of the term 'renegade' to describe some aspects of your old DNA may seem odd, but matters will become clearer to you as these older DNA frequencies become reactivated, and further aggregated by the energies passing through the Planet in conjunction with the Photon Belt. The purification of your DNA matrix, and the establishment of the dominant renegade DNA frequencies, will provide a collective harmonisation which will be irresistible. An appropriate analogy might be made between your DNA and sections of iron filings that are strewn in all directions on a piece of paper. As a magnet is drawn towards the iron filings, so there is a structured ordering of them according to the fields of energy being emitted by the magnet. The same is true of your renegade DNA sequences. The magnet in this case is Divine Love, and the energies are the fiery energies released by the Divine Father into the collective internal space of those who are willing and able to receive them. As the energies become progressively stronger, so it is that the old frequencies of all the Root Races that are encapsulated within your DNA, will come to the fore. DNA will no longer be silent[3] in the way that it is today, and many of the sequences that appear unconnected with normal biological functions will begin to become reactivated according to the harmonic frequency of Divine Light and Love.

So, the Solar Frequencies of the Divine Father will bring through a new octave of DNA realignment which will impact upon the physical, etheric, astral, and mental bodies of all those who are open to receiving these energies. The renegade DNA will open new doorways in the heart, and will send out a multi-component frequency signal which will span the older frequencies of planetary DNA, and will, in effect, reintroduce a whole host of new DNA frequencies into the human anatomy. What will be recognised, and what is already recognised by some, is that these older DNA frequencies will provide the physical bridges of intent to our star-brothers and sisters. These frequencies can — and will — only be opened by virtue of the high-frequency resonance that they will emit. They will only connect along specific bandwidths of intent, and they will act as keys to the space and substance of those extra-terrestrial connections, which represent the higher and more divine aspirations of our extra-terrestrial friends.

These connections will build upon, and blend with, those discussed earlier, but will differ in one significant aspect: they will provide a more potent means for total merging and realignment, on all levels, between us and our extra-terrestrial brothers and sisters. This will become clearer as we proceed.

Extra-Terrestrial Frequencies of Love and Light

The stellar frequencies, then, are providing a major backdrop for the ever-increasing vibrational energies which are currently bombarding your Planet. This stellar connection is extremely important, both in its impact and its intent, although you can only guess at this at the moment. The Solar Logos, as has been mentioned before, will play a key role in this transformation. However, the increased frequencies that are being utilised to grace your Planet, through the presence of your extra-terrestrial brothers and sisters, will also be of great consequence. It is the love frequencies which these extra-terrestrial friends are bringing which will provide a significant shift in your understanding, and in your attitude to your own development and transformation. It is of vital importance for you to connect with your extra-terrestrial heritage, and to acknowledge its role in Earth's development throughout all of the Root Races. Recognise also that these things have arisen through frequent interactions with your star-brothers and sisters.

This extra-terrestrial interaction spans the formation of Earth by the Creator Gods and their archetypes. It impinges upon the DNA imprinting of the Planet as a living library; upon the First Root Race, and its reliance on, and unfolding of, the magical qualities espoused in ancient wizardry, particularly the higher principles of love and light. The connection continued throughout the Second, Third, and Fourth Root Races, culminating in the Fifth Root Race. As the tides of communion between human beings and their extra-terrestrial brothers and sisters have ebbed and flowed through the ages, it is at the advent of the Sixth Root Race that a major transformation in this interaction will take place. You recognise that the scientific reasoning and elucidation of the last 150 years have produced great leaps in your understanding of the diversity of life on Earth. So it is that over the next thirty years or so, your minds and your energy systems will be prepared and expanded to receive the Divine Communication and Understanding which your extra-terrestrial brothers and sisters have learned and earned over the millennia.

This is a tremendous opportunity for you to compare notes, as it were: to exchange frequencies concerning your different experiences and understanding of the Divine nature of reality, and of how God is manifest in all things, both terrestrial and extra-terrestrial. You will discover that there is much in common between yourselves and your extra-terrestrial neighbours. It should come as no shock to you that the principles of love and light extend way beyond the boundaries of your solar system, your galaxy, and even your universe. Connecting with the new extra-terrestrial vibrations will allow you access to new information on levels unmatched throughout all of the Root Races to date. At the same time, you will be able to share your experiences of love and divinity, and to seed these experiences into other planets, other galaxies and other universes as part of the ongoing Divine Dialogue between many different life-forms. This connection will bring you all immense joy.

Accessing Stellar Frequencies and our Extra-Terrestrial Heritage

There are ways in which you can begin to build up this stellar connection, this new star frequency. Simply looking at the stars at night, and focusing on one that attracts you, will enable you to begin to connect with a stellar frequency. This initial connection will contribute to the clearing of your circuits, which is necessary at this time. Many of you feel a combination of fear and fascination toward things extra-terrestrial. For example, if you listen to the NASA recordings[4] of the Voyager spacecraft as it sped through your solar system, you may find that there are sections that attract you — where you feel 'at home' as it were. There may be other sections that make you feel more uncomfortable, and less able to 'handle' the vibrations. This is, regrettably, part and parcel of your ancestry, and it will be necessary to clear out these slower cordings and frequencies from the more dismal extra-terrestrial connections of the past.

So, *feel* into this diversity of emotional and physical responses that have been locked within your system over many ages. Allow yourself to connect, and to be led into a space where you can begin to appreciate that the time is rapidly approaching when a renaissance of communication with your extra-terrestrial friends will be necessary. This will happen on a number of different levels as you attune yourselves more and more profoundly.

The first level will be what is held in your body or tissue memory from lives gone by. This can be activated through looking at stars in the night sky. It can also be activated through meditation, and by feeling intuitively into different aspects of your physical vehicle. With time, what may emerge is an appreciation that your past extra-terrestrial connections have spanned the full spectrum of experiences, both light and dark. For some, these experiences may be held in different chakra centres and in different ways. For others, there may be a dim sense of the past, or a feeling, or a recognition. What really counts in this process is an appreciation of the range of different extra-terrestrial life-forms with which you have connected. Releasing the cordings from these past life experiences, particularly in the solar plexus and lower chakra centres, is extremely important.

Once this initial clearing has taken place, the second level of connection will begin. For those of you who have an extra-terrestrial heritage, it is likely that connections can be made easily with your star-brothers and sisters. The format and means by which this can happen will vary from person to person. These connections can be made most easily through meditation, and through what many of you call channelling[5]. The key is to *feel* into the vibration as it presents itself to you.

You will hold many preconceptions about what it is like to connect with extra-terrestrial frequencies, but ideally these should be laid aside, and your system left open to the experience. The connection that you will forge with your extra-terrestrial brothers and sisters will grow stronger and stronger. It will evolve into a deeper fellowship of understanding, a communion of minds and hearts, which will indeed be special, and very beautiful, in ways that go far beyond both your imagination and your comprehension.

Again, what matters here is a trust and acceptance of the reality that you *feel*. Too often, experiences and impressions are dismissed because they do not conform with someone's view or idea of reality. This stance will not allow you to access the broadest range of frequencies that you could potentially connect with. Ultimately, as you trust and connect more and more deeply, the possibility of direct telepathic communion can be expanded into a more physical linking whereby there is more of a merging between your own energy system and that of your extra-terrestrial brother or sister. This represents a further level of connection, and again, preconceptions of what it should or should not be like may well block the connection in the early stages. What should become clearer, as you explore these connections, is that the beauty and purity of the love will ascend more and more powerfully into your space. As these frequencies merge, true communion with your extra-terrestrial heritage will have taken place. As you feel these new connections, you will also awaken the divine within you, the divinity that resonates with your true essence, your true path and your true journey.

Sixth Root Race Reprise

The Sixth Root Race offers an unprecedented opportunity for light workers and heart workers throughout the Planet: a chance to connect so profoundly with their physical and spiritual heritage, that the veil of illusion, which has been so firmly held in place during the Fifth Root Race, will once and for all be cast aside. This new beginning, this new dawn of love and light, offers tremendous opportunities for spiritual growth, for harmonizing the huge array of frequencies both within and outside of the Planet. The Sixth Root Race will be a true merging of our hearts with the Divine within all of us, with the Divine Father and Mother, and with our extra-terrestrial heritage — which has been such a key component in the unfolding drama of our planetary, collective, and individual evolution.

This vast array of new frequencies will answer to the true calling of the heart — to the heart which is open, and which yearns for union with the Divine and to the heart which can embrace and trust the Sixth Root Race clarion-call of 'unity through diversity'. You have the capacity and the authority to access this new wave of energy which is entering your Planet so forcefully, as part of the Father's Will and Authority. The twin frequencies of love and light, which span the multiple octaves of these new energies, will be your true guides to the Divine, and your true guides of the heart. They will unlock the keys to your heart — safely, securely, and according to the Divine Plan and to your own personal needs. All you need do is to trust, to bring in the Paramatman Light, and to know that the Father's Will is being done. This is especially so during these times, when the energies and the developments on the Planet appear to be so at odds with what has been promised in the ascendancy of the Sixth Root Race.

However, as the symbol of Divine Service is forged on the innermost recesses of your heart, and the rhythm of a new regime of Divine Infiltrations echoes within the vastness of your soul, know that true and lasting peace can be found within the keys to your heart. It is all there. The multiple doorways of Divine Longing are being unlocked, and the path to your true home, to your true, natural state, in the one, never-ending reality, is guaranteed by the Divine Hierarchy of Avatars and Perfect Masters.

Know that all is as it should be, and that you are loved more than you can possibly imagine, and that you have the Divine within you, irrespective of who you are, and no matter what your nationality, creed, or colour. The Divine knows no boundaries within these representations, neither terrestrially nor extra-terrestrially.

So: trust in the unfolding, trust in the grand adventure, and trust that your path home is secure; that you are immortal, and that your separation from your true divinity is nothing more than an illusion. This knowledge will, in time, become clearer and clearer, like a beacon of brilliant light. The transition from the Fifth Root Race to the Sixth Root Race is well underway. Patience, trust, love, and light will ensure that you never lose your way.

Chapter 9 • Blazing the Trail

Blazing a Trail to the Divine
Cultivating Patience and Trust
Points of Light

After all that has been said so far, one may well ask how the emergence of the Sixth Root Race will come about: how can such a transformation, at all levels, take place in such a short space of time? How can a balance be maintained in the turbulent times ahead? How can these new frequencies be anchored effectively into the Planet, and into the space of all living beings? These are important questions. Some of the background and answers have already been given, but it is as well to spell out clearly the various processes by which all light workers, and ultimately all living beings, can ascend in their frequencies. There will, inevitably, be casualties in this process. Some people will be overcome by fear and by depression, and will be unable to access the new frequencies. These individuals have already, on one level, made the choice to go home, and will be doing so more collectively over the coming years.

The fundamental point concerns the new frequency-rapport that is demanded by the Sixth Root Race, and which has been instigated by the Avataric Network. Everything will proceed according to the Divine Plan, and will be unfolded through the Avataric Agency. This is the first and most important point. The second point is that Sixth Root Race living is not based upon the needs of the individual, but rather on the collective love and light manifested through the group and the Mind of One. It is only through combining collectively that each individual can clear out the older, slower frequencies of past life traumas and present life difficulties, and access the new frequencies.

The third point is that through meditation and other techniques, it is possible to connect multi-dimensionally, and to begin raising one's vibration to a new frequency. The call should be, at all times, to connect with the Paramatman Light, and to connect with the Divine within all through your hearts. Trust in the Divine, trust in the light, and trust in God. All will be taken care of, although living in this mode will require a 180° turn away from your present ways of living and behaving. This will be part of the challenge.

The fourth and final point is to see the current planetary changes as real gateways of opportunity for all living beings. To come from the heart with joy and happiness, and to anchor the light within yourselves and the Planet, is to fulfil your true destiny as light workers

During this process, there will be many who will seek to bring your frequency vibration down to a lower level, to engage you in the grosser aspects of mind abuse, and to ensure that you remain anchored within the older survivalistic frequencies. These attempts must be brushed aside: keep your intent firmly fixed on the Divine play of new frequencies as they enter your space. *This* is what matters. You will, in every sense of the word, be blazing a new trail for all to follow. There will be highs and lows, and there will also be stern challenges that will test your intent, and your new-found will, to the very foundations of your being. This is a necessary part of the transformation. In such times of turmoil, it is advisable to trust in the process, to remember that even in the midst of the turbulence, you are directly anchored to the Divine. Trust in the Divine, and nothing can touch you or deflect you from your path.

Blazing a Trail to the Divine

Connect with all your heart
With the Divine Fire within you.
Feel the intent of Love and Light.
Feel the glowing embers of Divine Light.
Ignite the Fire and Knowledge within you.
Find your way home.

Trust your Divine Companion on this epic journey.
Realise that God is with you each step of the way;
To Him no step is too great,
No distance covered too much,
No burden too heavy.
Feel the light of your Soul, the light of your destiny,
Illumine the path in front of you
To be the guiding light on your journey home.

For whence has your Soul come?
And where shall it go?
All rivers are but part of the Divine Ocean of Light.
Your journey is long and hard,
But know that Divine Love knows all pains, all joys —
For the journey home is the journey of the Beloved.

It is the journey of the Divine,
The wellspring of eternal bliss,
The wellspring of eternal peace,
For this is your Soul's destiny:
To be a piece of the Divine,
And through that piece to become the Divine.

This is your journey's promise,
This is your journey's end:
To become Divine,
To love God,
To love the Divine
As God loves you.
So shall you entwine.

The trail embraces many different levels on both the physical and the inner planes. In effect, you must blaze a trail from the lower astral planes up into the higher mental planes. If you could see the length of the trail and the degree of effort required to make this journey, you would be amazed. You must cross so many planes, and move through so many different frequency-notes — often in a chameleon-like way, so that you blend in with the respective energy levels. You will be beating an upward path through these levels, working your way towards the Light. It is of paramount importance, for it is in blazing this trail to the Avatar's doorway that you will realise your own divinity.

Cultivating Patience and Trust

As with any long journey, there are many obstacles, there are many potential pitfalls, and there are the highs and lows. The pitfalls are often in the mind, although for some people they do have a physical presence. They include over-confidence, lack of self-worth, a deep fear of the unknown, and a sense that to trust is tantamount to letting go of your right to choose. All of these problems are encountered by those on the path to the Divine. There is also the very real threat of being affected by slower-frequency energies, which can lower your vibration, and prevent you from seeing the bigger picture. To blaze this trail through the planes, to become flexible in travelling between the astral and mental planes, you must have commit-ment, courage, and — above all — patience. Many, many light workers are impatient to see results immediately, but this does not usually transpire and so patience has to be cultivated: patience in the unfolding of everything, in the appropriate manner and at the appropriate time.

Blazing a trail also means 'breaking the mould' with your family and friends, and wishing above all else to change, and to find your true heart keys, which will resonate and vibrate with your true essence on the inner planes. For many people, this will be difficult to comprehend, and so it is that patience and trust are again required in large measure, to counteract the views of others: do not be swayed by the opinions of those who may think that you are going in the wrong direction. There will be times when you will feel isolated, confronting, within this isolation, your true abyss. In crossing the abyss, from third-dimensional thinking to fourth-dimensional and multi-dimensional experience, there are many old ties and thought forms that will need to be broken and disconnected from. It is often an emotionally difficult time, but this initiation process is necessary, because it will help balance and toughen you for the path ahead. It is through a recognition of the juxtaposition between the isolation and the collective, that you can fully appreciate the power and the beauty of the group.

So while it may appear as if you are alone, in truth you are not; and this shift in perception can provide an opportunity to cultivate deeper connections with your guides on the inner planes. This cleansing process is also a requirement for the removal of old karma which may slow your progress or hinder your development. All of these aspects are part of the inner path which you must follow in order to achieve the shift from your solar plexus to your heart. Many will not understand this process within themselves at first, but as time passes, you will come to see the relevance of the preparation and effort that you have invested in your spiritual quest.

Points of Light

Part of the challenge will lie in seeking the points of light that can help to illuminate your way forward along the path. There are various aspects to this exercise, some of which we have touched on in earlier chapters. In sum, though, in terms of inner-planes progress, the key is in turning to the light, and

> seeking it out at all times. As you invoke this Divine Light, It will help to bring you closer to your home, closer to your own light. It should be invoked to fill you on every level, both conscious and unconscious.

The expression, 'points of light' also refers to the different light levels within our own being, which need to be accessed during our journey to the Divine. Only a few of our lives can truly be described as points of blinding light and beauty, lives such as we all aspire to within ourselves. We may have no conscious memory of having lived these lives, but the information is stored in our akashic records[1]. So, in seeking the points of light on our soul's journey, it is as if we now have the opportunity, to create another point of light, another star of great beauty, another life of love and service to the Divine. These points of light are rare. To aspire to them and to realise them we must blaze a trail to the Divine, and connect with the light as much as possible, and all the time. It means that the love and light frequencies that we irradiate and transmit must be of the purest note that we can attain. So, as we progress along this path, we pour out more light, we take in more light, and our overall capacity to handle and hold more light increases exponentially.

The initiation of the Sixth Root Race *is* one of these special points of light, a point among many occurring throughout our journeys through eternity. What is different today is that we must blaze the trail within ourselves, through our own invocation and also through the Great Invocation, to bring into reality, this life of light, this point of light, which we are all destined to become.

Epilogue

It has been our pleasure to connect with you, dear reader, in this experiment. We do not expect you to believe all that has been said, nor do we expect you to agree with what has been expressed. All we hope is that you will have had the opportunity to feel with your heart, to feel into the energy that we present to you in these pages. If you have felt some connection in your heart during this process, then we shall have achieved what we set out to do, which was simply to connect, and to allow a seed of opportunity to form in your hearts. For this, we thank you.

Please be assured that this is not a one-way process. Communication and communing are always parts of a two-way process, and just as our energies have reached out across different dimensions, so it is that the resonant responses of your hearts will reach back to us. Invoke with love, invoke with light, and all that you have connected with in these words can become a more vibrant reality. We are indeed privileged and delighted to be a part of this grand experiment. Feel free to call upon us at any time, in any place. Look into your hearts and feel our pulse beat; hear our call of love, our call of communication. As you connect more deeply, you will begin to feel the true rapport of hearts and minds. We have many names, but principal amongst us is Baluthra, of the Dragon tribe. We would be privileged and delighted if you would call upon us.

With love and light.
Baluthra and friends.

Notes on the Chapters

Chapter I

1. **Body energy** in this context not only refers to the physical aspect of the body, but also to the subtle anatomy (see *Note 3* below) composed of much finer energies.

2. **Cartesian split** refers to the split between the mind and body first put forward by Rene Descartes in the 17th Century. Descartes is famous for stating "Cogito ergo sum" — "I think, therefore, I am". Traditional western thinking has subsequently focused on the separation between the mind and body, and on how the mind controls the body. This somewhat artificial split has formed the basis for subsequent dualistic thinking in philosophy and science.

3. **The subtle anatomy** refers to a series of interconnecting and interpenetrating bodies which are not usually visible to the naked eye but which can be 'sensed' with practice. The first of these is known as the etheric body, which is an energy sheath that extends out to about an inch off the body. It can sometimes be seen as a whitish light surrounding a person's body. The polarity of the etheric body is the opposite of a person's gender. So in women, the etheric will be more masculine in energy, while in men it will be more feminine. **The aura** is a larger, subtle body which sheaths the whole physical body. In a healthy person it should surround them for between five and six metres. It is composed of a fine mesh of electromagnetic energies that pulse and radiate different light frequencies and colours. The aura will directly reflect the state of a person's health. In modern society, with so much electromagnetic energy present, the aura is often clogged up with static and damaged.

4. **Involution** refers to the process whereby the consciousness of the soul gradually disengages from the physical or gross world and turns inward. During the first six planes, the soul gradually withdraws from the focus of its consciousness from the gross sphere to

the subtle sphere and then to the mental sphere (see also *Planes of Consciousness*). This is involution. At the seventh plane the soul experiences Realisation and knows itself to be God. Meher Baba discussed involution in depth in *God Speaks*.

5. **Evolution** refers to the progressive evolution of consciousness from the stone stage through the plant and animal kingdom, culminating in man. The history of evolution is the gradual development of consciousness.

6. **The planetary vibration** represents the sum total of Earth's frequency as manifested on the physical, astral, and mental planes. In physical terms, the Earth has been found to pulse electromagnetically. This electromagnetic pulse is the fundamental heart beat of the Earth and for every one second in linear time, the Earth was found to pulse at 7.8 beats per second. Recent measurements of this pulse beat show that it is increasing rapidly.

7. **Scientific orthodoxy** refers to physical **DNA**, which is the physical structure of nucleotide bases linked by sugar-phosphate groups in a double helix arrangement. The ordering of the nucleotide bases, as rungs of the ladder within the helix, forms the basis of genetic information. In describing **subtle DNA**, I am referring to a deeper level, a pattern of interrelationship between vibration and matter which is manifested in light particles. All experience is recorded within these particles which comprise the DNA. Although our subtle DNA stranding is made up of two strands, there is a shift now occurring where this level can be increased towards six main pairs of DNA stranding. See also *Note 15* below.

8. **The ajna centre** is located at the back of the head, adjacent to the part of the brain known as the medulla oblongata. The medulla oblongata forms part of the brain stem which is connected to the spinal chord. The ajna centre is in line with the top of the upper lip on the face. It is usually a connection point for communication with our inner guides.

9. The term **'Divine Beings'** is used in a specific sense here to cover God-Realised Beings, Perfect Masters, the Avatar, and those beings on the inner planes who are highly evolved. It is also true that we

are all divine in the sense that we are each an aspect of God, although we do not yet realise it. This latter sense is not implied in this context. See also *The Avatar, Perfect Master*.

10. In *The Selfish Gene* (1976, Oxford University Press), Richard Dawkins set out the position that the basic unit of evolution is the gene and that it is the survival of the gene which is most important in explaining evolutionary phenomena including behaviour.

11. **'Connecting with the group'** means invoking a link through a centre of your choice, such as the heart chakra, with light workers and those working with the Divine. In practice, this connection is most easily established through meditation, by calling in the group and representing that connection within the heart centre by a golden disc or some other intuitive symbol. Connecting with the group will immediately raise your frequency vibration.

12. **The Avataric Network** refers to the Avatar in His various forms, and all of His physical incarnations, past, present, and future. It includes, to name but a few Avatars, the Christ, the Buddha, and Lord Krishna. The Network also encompasses those Divine Beings embodying or working directly with Avataric Energies, or other aspects of the Avatar, and include Sathya Sai Baba, Babaji, and Mother Meera.

13. **The Spiritual Hierarchy** is a grouping of seven thousand individuals who form a bridge between Shamballa (a centre where divine energy streams out) and humanity. Their function is to step-down the frequencies released from Shamballa so that the light and information can be more easily digested by humanity in general. All members of the Spiritual Hierarchy are currently in incarnation on Earth

14. **God-realisation** is when the soul experiences itself as God. God-realisation is a unique state of consciousness because it is not dependent upon the individual mind or any other medium. Achieving God-Realisation requires the emancipation of consciousness from the limitations of mind. There are fifty-six God-Realised beings in the world at all times and they are always one in consciousness.

15. **Renegade DNA** refers to an ancient type of DNA. Some 300,000 years ago, the human race underwent a reduction in its DNA stranding from nine to two. The aspect of DNA that escaped this stripping down, and which has remained within the human race, is referred to as renegade DNA. This renegade DNA is now being actively integrated into the essence of various people, so that the memory of what has happened within the human race as a whole can be recalled. It is important to recognise that DNA, as a sequence of energy and information, can act as a memory reservoir. As the old DNA lineage is restored, then the older frequencies can be reintegrated and allow a greater structural identification within the human race as a whole, to take place.

16. For example, the Dolphins. See Chapter III.

17. **The Divine Ocean** is the Source, or the formation of God. See also *Note 20* (Chapter II) below.

18. **Maya** is the principle of illusion or ignorance. Maya is not illusion, but rather the creator of illusion; it is not duality, but the creator of duality.

19. These **frequency 'packets'** represent collectives of individual energy or thought forms which tend to vibrate at the lower end of the spectrum and which, therefore, seek to maintain a matrix of distrust which supports this slower vibration. A different grouping of these frequency 'packets' are known as energy pirates. Energy pirates are an intelligence which have a vested interest in receiving energy patterns from sources external to themselves. The energy pirate operates on the inner planes and has the capacity to move from plane to plane in search of energy that it can then negotiate in other planes of existence.

Chapter II

1. **Crystal skulls** can be positively or negatively charged, reflecting light or dark aspects.

2. **Time lines** exist physically, astrally, and mentally, and are inter-dimensional frequencies which operate within a particular time

period. These time periods can be past, present, or future and for an individual soul aspect will be held in place by karma. So a soul aspect can incarnate within a particular time-line to work through karma. Although time only exists linearly within a physical framework, it is possible for an individual to work with future time-lines and past time-lines while in the present, although this does require some practice and expertise.

3. **The abyss** represents a point in a person's spiritual development where it may appear to that person that they are confronted by an abyss, whether it be mentally, emotionally, or physically. In these instances, the individual may feel completely alone and have to find a way to move through the perceived difficulty. The purpose of confronting an abyss is to cultivate trust, and enable the individual to grow stronger from such experiences. While we may feel that we have confronted an abyss in the physical sense, such abysses also exist on the inner planes.

4. The more common use is the **mental planes**, since 'causal' can have different interpretations.

5. **The Paramatma** is the Supreme Self, The Absolute, the Supreme Divine Being.

6. **The greys** are a race of extra-terrestrials so called because of their skin colour and their connection to abduction experiences of many people. The greys represent a particularly low frequency that is no longer applicable to the new energies entering the Planet.

7. **DNA length** does not initially refer to the physical level, but rather more to our subtle DNA and its harmonisation to accommodate extra-long frequencies. Of course once the changes have been implemented on the subtle levels, then the physical counterpart will eventually emerge.

8. **The body-plan** of an organism defines its basic blueprint. For example, the body plan of an animal can be bipedal (as in humans), radial (as in a starfish), or coelomic (as in a worm). Plants and minerals also have blueprints, although in the latter it is a crystalline blueprint. It is also possible to go below this phenotypic expression

(i.e. physical appearance) and look at the DNA blueprint. This will then relate to the arrangement of genes, how they are expressed in development, and so on.

9. Although we recognise that our brain has a **'reptilian'** component that describes the 'lower' brain functions such as body homeostasis, in this context we are really referring to our extra-terrestrial past-life experiences when we were reptiles. This reptilian connection is an ancient one.

10. When soul aspects enter the physical planes they will sometimes come in unprepared, or too rapidly, and find that they are out of step with what they agreed to undertake before coming down. They may fail to meet the appropriate people at a given time or simply have lost the connection with their inner family. If this happens over many lifetimes, then the memory of what they needed to do becomes lost, and the process of recall can be difficult and require assistance.

11. **Existentialism** is a philosophical attitude which is generally opposed to rationalist and empiricist doctrines which assume that the universe is a determined, ordered system intelligible to the contemplative observer. Such an observer can discover the natural laws that govern all beings and the role of reason as the power guiding human activity. In existentialism, the problem of being must take precedence over that of knowledge in philosophical investigations. Being cannot be made a subject of objective enquiry; it is revealed to the individual by reflection on his own unique concrete existence in time and space. Existence is, therefore, basic and it is the fact of the individual's presence and participation in a changing world. Exponents of the existentialist movement included Heidegger and Sartre.

12. **Mechanism** is a scientific philosophy developed principally by Descartes in which mechanical principles based on shape, size, and motions are used to define the world and all that is contained in it. Apart from also rejecting any qualitative analysis of objects, mechanism rejects any notion of purposes or teleological explanations in its scientific analysis.

13. **Holism** is founded on the principle that wholes, or some wholes, are more than the sum of their parts. In some examples, holism focuses on a world view where the whole cannot be understood just in terms of its parts, but should be analysed in terms of the whole, whether it be in relation to structures or functions.

14. **Dadaism** is a literary or artistic movement of the period 1916-1922. It proclaimed the intention to replace rationality with deliberate madness, and chaos in art.

15. **Veda** is a general term for scriptures of Hindusim. The oldest, the Rig-Veda, includes around 1,000 hymns in praise of gods. The philosophical writings forming commentaries of the Veda, including the Upsanishads, are known as the Vedanta. They hold that ultimate reality is not accessible to experience but only to direct intuition.

16. **Conceptual** refers to the notion that general or abstract terms have meaning because they name or refer to corresponding non-physical entities, called concepts. Some concepts may be powerful thinking tools even when they are not fully understood. The most extreme version of the conceptual view is that concepts can refer to mental images.

17. **A hologram** is a three-dimensional image which has been generated by a light source, typically a laser. A hologram is scalable and importantly, any part of the hologram contains the whole image. Thus, in describing a holographic attitude, one could say that it encompassed a view where, for example, everything is connected to everything else, where each part contains the whole, and where consciousness is the basic reality. Holographic approaches are being developed in new healing approaches where dis-ease is seen as the result of a distortion in our consciousness and a block in our connection to the Source.

18. **The Heisenberg uncertainty principle** relates to the position and velocity of a particle. One can never be exactly sure of both the position and velocity of a particle; the more accurately one knows the one, the less accurately one can know the other.

19. **Darwinian evolution** is based on the premise that genetic varia-
tion within populations of organisms is subject to selective pres-
sures and that permanent changes arise within populations through
mutation. Over time, this combination of selective pressure and
mutation leads to the emergence of new species. Darwinian evolution basically means descent with modification, usually in a gradual
and incremental manner.

20. When the soul is at the Source, within God, it is part of the 'Divine
Ocean' which is the unity of everything. Within the Divine Ocean
there occurs an ongoing process of vibrationary changes which
whip up the atmosphere. This atmosphere, or **Breath of the
Creator,** separates off from the Ocean small droplets of divinity.

21. **Sri Aurobindo** was a great Indian yogi and philosopher of recent
times, who lived in Pondicherry, India. He was the author of a
number of metaphysical masterpieces, including *The Life Divine*. He
also taught yoga.

Chapter III

1. **Invoking Highest Good** is rather like a safety mechanism for all
that you invoke. By invoking Highest Good, you are trusting in the
Divine and ensuring that your personality choices or vested interests do not cloud your invocation. For example, asking for help or
healing according to Highest Good will ensure that the request is
assessed through the highest frequency input.

2. **The system** here refers to the expression of the Divine on every
level, both on the outer and inner planes. Another way of describing the system is 'working with Light'.

3. **Bovine Spongiform Encepalopathy (BSE)** is a disease that
affects cattle and is caused by prions, which infect nerve cells.

4. Over the last 600 million years, there have been a number of **mass
extinctions,** the most famous of which was at the end of the
Cretaceous Period (about 70 million years ago) when the dinosaurs
and many other life forms were wiped out by an asteroid colliding

with the Planet. There have been a number of earlier extinctions in the Earth's history which had a similarly dramatic effect on the diversity of life.

5. These come under the general categories of fear, greed, selfishness, feudalism, and violence.

6. See also *Note 9* below. **Planetary frequency holders** refers to those individuals who have the capacity, internal space, and DNA structure to hold and resonate with the vast array of frequencies held within the Planet. This can include all the different types of life forms, both Devic and Elemental, as well as the DNA frequencies held and expressed by the plant and animal kingdoms.

7. **The phenotype** of an organism is its appearance — its morphology, physiology, and ways of life — what we can observe. This is distinct from the genotype, which is the sum total of hereditary materials of the organism. The phenotype changes continuously throughout the life of an organism, from the moment of conception to its death.

8. **Homology** refers to correspondence or similarity of features in different organisms due to inheritance from a common ancestor. For example, the forelimbs of dogs, whales, and chickens are homologous; the skeletons of these limbs are all constructed of bones arranged according to the same pattern because they were inherited from an ancestor with similarly arranged forelimbs.

9. **Living librarians** refer to those souls who have been present in matter since the seeding of the DNA frequencies into the Planet and who have the capacity to merge and reflect, within their internal space, these original frequencies. The original frequencies cover all life forms on the Planet at present, and those that have gone before through each of the Root Races. By holding and transmitting these DNA frequencies, these collective accords of frequencies, the 'librarians' act as reference points of information.

10. **Lion people** are extra-terrestrials who inhabit a different planetary structure from us. Lion people are time masters and have mastered time within our third-dimensional reality as we perceive it,

and have the capacity to work within different time frequencies. Physically they have the appearance of lions although they stand upright on two feet. They operate on the inner planes, although some of them have physically incarnated in the past. References to these Lion people can be found in ancient cultures, such as in the Egyptian period, through statues and artefacts. The Lion people are sometimes referred to as Passchats.

11. **The Dragon tribes** are another group of extra-terrestrials, who occupy a different dimensional stream of consciousness. They operate on the inner planes and are actively involved in facilitating the current changes on the Planet. Their appearance on the inner planes is similar to that of dragons from mythology, with feet, wings, long tails, and necks. Their frequencies are a direct expression of love and power, and within each Dragon tribe there are different frequencies reflecting their collective foci. Dragon guides will often work directly with the heart.

12. **The Reptilian frequencies** represent a past-life extra-terrestrial connection. Part of the fragmentation in frequencies and interference that occurred on the Planet in the past has been due to extra-terrestrial reptilian frequencies. As viewed from the energy levels present in the Planet today, the reptiles exhibit slower frequencies. There are several different reptilian groupings and the time has come for a balancing of the karmic ties with these frequencies.

13. **The Pleiadians** are a collective extra-terrestrial grouping, originating in the Pleiades, who are interacting with a number of different people on Earth. Again, they inhabit a different dimensional reality, operate on the inner planes, and are focusing a different grouping of energies into the Planet. A number of different books have been written about them and details can be found in the Bibliography.

14. **The Sirian White Lodge** are high frequency energy beings who work entirely with Light, with the karmic laws, both on the inner and outer planes and have their point of origin in Sirius.

15. **The Amphibian frequencies** are again an extra-terrestrial grouping from a different dimensional reality.

16. **The Insects** manifest a collective system or society and the reference in this context is to extra-terrestrial frequencies. Since every living form on Earth is duplicated elsewhere within the Galaxy, the presence of Planets inhabited by collective intelligences working within the insect archetype or body plan should not be a complete shock. Although much larger than those present on Earth, the appearance of these insects is similar to what we see on Earth. Again, these frequencies also operate on the inner planes and can be accessed there.

17. Like the Insect frequencies, the **Spider frequencies** have an extra-terrestrial reference point and can be accessed through the inner planes. The Spider frequencies also operate on a more collective basis and some of the frequencies which they embody can be very beautiful and provide a strong heart connection.

18. **Ancestral lineage** refers to the DNA mix that is passed down through thousands of generations from both the female and male sides of the family. This DNA mix will be an expression of the experiences held in matter by our ancestors.

19. **Family focus** refers to the skills and interests of one's physical family, i.e. the environment a child grows up in. However, it is possible to have a family focus on the inner planes, such as with one's soul family.

20. These refer to different frequencies which have been seeded in the mental planes and which will become activated by specific energy alignments. A good example would be the activation of a Crystal Skull, where a particular Skull may remain dormant until activated by the correct mental frequency which effectively opens a new doorway or alignment. Some of the older sacred sites on the Planet have been seeded in the past and will be activated in the near future by the appropriate mix and level of energy.

21. At the physical level, the development of an organism is determined by complex networks of interactions between gene products. As an organism develops, **gene switches** inside cells are activated and lead to the development of different cell types. This is a complex process and specific developmental genes are activated for

specific periods of time and then de-activated. For development to proceed properly, these activated genes need to receive appropriate stimuli which set in motion the next stage of growth.

22. **Karmic cordings** are lines of energy between individuals, and in effect represent a restriction of energy movement or expression. These cordings are often between the various chakra centres and are a reflection of past life experiences. Clearing these cordings is an important process in raising one's vibration and removing slower frequencies which can hold one back.

23. Since linear time is only manifested on the physical planes and is, therefore, an illusion from the perspective of the astral and mental planes, it is possible for past and future aspects of oneself to manifest in one's inner space at a given point in linear time. The processes of death and rebirth, and the frequency of time, allow individuals to explore their karmic patterns and exercise their personal choice. It is in this sense that death and time are **karmic points** of reference.

24. **Trance channels** are individuals who offer their physical space for use by different frequencies and energies. Typically, a trance channel will have spent a long time in apprenticeship, involving the development of a better astral and mental alignment and the removal of unwanted thought forms. By the appropriate use of the will, it becomes possible to allow guides and different frequencies into one's internal space, so that those on the inner planes wishing to offer a different information flow to the human race can do so. Trance channelling is a deeper form of channelling than 'overshadowing' or telepathic channelling where the subtle body of an individual may communicate telepathically with an intelligence on the inner planes, or may merge with them.

25. **Alcyone** is situated in the constellation of Taurus, as are the Pleiades. Alcyone is the brightest star in the constellation, some 1000 times brighter than our Sun and ten times larger.

26. See *Note 17* (Chapter II) for a description of the term **'holographic'**. The sense implied here is that the Paramatman Light is the Light source for the hologram, or the muli-dimensional image.

Chapter IV

1. **'Earthing'** in this context means holding and transmitting the new energies into the Earth. Part of this process requires the clearance of old astral energy as well as the need for an individual to be properly 'grounded', or present in their body. This requires that a person is properly in their body and is able to bring in their power, receive clear guidance, and have the ability to receive direct information.

2. These can sometimes be visualised as an area of thinning in the **etheric body** and will include areas where energy is not free-flowing.

3. **Static** is electric charge at rest and is often produced by friction or induction.

4. These are the energies of the earth, and it is possible to tap into the female essence of the Earth in meditation, and to draw the Earth's energy into one's body.

5. **The signal or frequency-signature** can refer to different types of energy which need to be accessed, including specific information from guides, or specific light frequencies which a person has the authority to access.

6. **The central doorkeeper** is the main guide on the inner planes who oversees an individual's programme from the inner planes. The central doorkeeper will orchestrate interactions with other guides and also be responsible for which guides have closer access to that person. Since guides come in many different shapes and sizes, and with different degrees of experience, it is important that the central doorkeeper is experienced and powerful.

7. There are a number of different ways of doing this. Generally, connecting with our guidance requires practice through meditation and patience. David Cousin's book *A Handbook for Light Workers* describes a number of different meditations for connecting to and working with guides. Generally speaking, when you connect with **your inner guidance**, you will feel an inner expansion, a sense of well-being, and often a sense of the familiar. With practice, it becomes possible to feel your guides more specifically and forcefully.

8. Within a group setting, there will be a spectrum of **karmic connections** between the participants. This diversity allows greater flexibility within a group so that a person can individually and collectively renegotiate their karma, and in so doing, drive up the collective frequency of the group. In other words, old contracts and slower frequency bondings can be released.

9. **Sathya Sai Baba** was born in 1926 in southern India, and proclaimed himself the reincarnation of Sai Saba of Shirdi (1835-1918) while in his teens. Known for His miraculous powers and His ability to transform and heal the hearts of people, Sathya Sai Baba's central message is based on the Unity of Faiths and the importance of Love as the principal human value for all humanity to live by. He is regarded as the second of a tri-incarnation — the first being Sai Baba of Shirdi. Prema Sai Baba, the third incarnation, is predicted to come after Sathya Sai Baba. See also Chapter V.

10. **Merwan Sheriar Irani** was born in Poona, India on 25 February 1894. In 1913 He was awakened to His true status as the Avatar, the total manifestation of God in human form, by Hazrat Babajan, one of the five Perfect Masters of the time. Merwan subsequently met the Perfect Master Sai Baba of Shirdi — who in turn guided Him to another of the Perfect Masters, Upasni Maharaj, a Hindu, in Sakori. His Avataric mission started its outward expression in 1921 with the gathering together of His first disciples, who gave Him the name *Meher Baba*, which means "Compassionate Father". Meher Baba set up residence near Ahmednagar, India at a place which became known as Meherabad. Meher Baba travelled extensively in India and also took a vow of silence in 1925 which remained unbroken until the time of His passing away on 31 January 1969. Meher Baba often stated "I come not to teach but to awaken". See also the Bibliography for references to Meher Baba's life and teachings.

11. **The 'Unspoken Word'** refers in one aspect, to the Word that Meher Baba will speak when He breaks His Silence. During His Life, there was much speculation as to when he would break His Vow of Silence. In another sense, the 'Unspoken Word' refers to the timing and sequencing of the releases of the new waves of

energies by Meher Baba integral to the transformation into the Sixth Root Race.

12. This is another term for God the Creator.

13. The different sensory stimuli to which we react — tactile, visual, auditory, olfactory, etc. — are produced by vibratory variations in electrons and protons. The vibrations in turn are regulated by **prana** — subtle life-forces of energies finer than atomic energies. Prana is life force energy.

14. This condition is sometimes referred to as 'sleep paralysis'.

15. **Slower-frequency vibrations** are present on the lower planes, generally the zero, first, and second planes. Situations where people feel these emotions for periods of time, without necessarily understanding why, are indicators that they have stationed their awareness in the lower planes. As the astral levels become completely open, it is important to be able to build an inner awareness of what plane-setting you may be on, so that a better perspective can be obtained, as well as developing an ability to alter your plane-setting at will.

16. **The Devic Kingdom**, like the Mineral Kingdom, refers to the collective grouping of all Devas, in whatever form they present themselves.

17. **A ray** is a particular force or type of energy, with particular emphasis on its qualities, rather than its form. **Ray types** refer to the Seven Rays of Life, which are direct emanations from God and which embody different qualities, e.g. Love, Will, or Intelligence.

18. This is like having a key which can open a door, except the key is a specific frequency and the door may, for example, be a dimensional doorway, or access to a guide.

19. In **polar wandering**, the magnetic poles move around the true poles. This movement around both the North and South Poles occurs in a cyclical manner and at present the magnetic North Pole is about 7° off from the true North Pole.

20. **Geomagnetic reversals** arise when the magnetic poles swap over, so that the North Pole becomes the South Pole and vice versa. These reversals can be found in the magnetic orientation of minerals in rocks which, like tree rings, can offer a blueprint of the polar orientation over millions of years. Geomagnetic reversals are often associated with minor extinctions of plant and animal species.

Chapter V

1. **God-Head** or **God-Force** refers, in this context, to the direct descent of God on Earth as the Avatar and is the independent status of God when God directly becomes man without undergoing or passing through the process of evolution, reincarnation, and involution of consciousness. It is God with infinite attributes.

2. Other **Avatars** include The Buddha, Zoroaster, Abraham, and Hercules.

3. **Sai Baba of Shirdi** (1838-1918) was the Head of the Spiritual Hierarchy and the leading Perfect Master of his time.

4. **Mother Meera** was born in India in 1960 and now lives in Germany. Mother Meera is a Divine Mother and during Darshan bestows Paramatman Light.

5. **The Divine Mother, Ammachi,** is a Perfect Master.

6. Previous examples of Perfect Masters include Tajuddin Baba and Narayan Maharaj, who along with Sai Baba of Shirdi, Upasni Maharaj, and Hazrat Babajan, comprised the five Perfect Masters who called the Avatar into physical incarnation. The Iranian poet Hafiz (Shams-ud-din Muahammad Hafiz), who wrote in the 14th Century, was also a Perfect Master as was Rumi, the 13th-century Perfect Master who founded the Mevlevi ('whirling') dervishes.

7. **Universal Work** means working for the Divine and according to the Divine Plan both in the physical and on the inner planes.

8. In the past, religions have acted as intermediaries between individuals and God. Because a religion always interprets the words and actions of the Avatar, they will inevitably **step-down** the original frequency of the Avatar.

9. This quote was made by Meher Baba.

10. **Sanskaras** are impressions or accumulated imprints of past experiences (including past lives) which determine one's desires and actions in the present lifetime.

11. **Adepts** are those who are proficient in a spiritual sense and have reached a certain level of attainment on the inner planes.

12. **The Kundalini** is the vital force, or power, residing near the base of the spine, represented symbolically as a coiled cobra. Kundalini can also mean 'fire'.

13. **The medulla** is located in the brain stem and is responsible for maintaining the rate of heart contraction, blood pressure, and breathing rate.

14. **The sphenoid bone** is a butterfly shaped bone that is located in the floor of the cranium.

15. For example, the thyroid glands, the adrenal glands, the ovaries, and the testes.

16. **The pineal gland** is located in the middle of the brain and is involved in regulating the sleep-wake cycle.

17. **The five-pointed star** is an ancient symbol which can act as a protective vibration for your help.

18. **Point singularity** is a region of space-time where physical variables become infinite, such as density, tidal forces, and pressure.

19. **Psychometrising** literally means to divine or determine from physical contact or close physical proximity the quality of an object or a person.

20. This refers to the different **plane levels** mentioned before. It is useful exercise to practice focusing on the plane level, first by subdividing the planes into seven, and then further subdividing each plane into ten. Each of these tenths can then be further subdivided if so wished. So, for example, it can be helpful to determine the plane level of channelled information, or the plane level at which a

guide is operating from. This can be done by tapping into the energy source and then intuitively giving it a plane level, and then further sub-dividing this number.

21. **Occult** means 'beyond the range of ordinary experience', or 'that which is hidden or concealed'.

22. Only a small number of **Crystal Skulls** have been located to date, although it is possible to access some of the Crystal Skull frequencies on the inner planes. It is said that these Skulls will be accessed on the physical plane once they are ready to be found.

Chapter VI

1. **The Great Invocation** was released into humanity in the 1930's and can be used irrespective of background or creed. It is a dominant energy package of the Cosmic Christ and so working with the Great Invocation can boost one in a high frequency way.

2. The books of **Alice Bailey** and the Tibetan, **Djwhal Khul,** are the direct result of a collaboration between a working disciple and a member of the Spiritual Hierarchy. A wide range of books have been channelled by Alice Bailey on the Tibetan's teachings, and a selection is given in the Bibliography.

3. **Light** representing different types of vibration and inherent qualities.

4. See *The Seven Rays of Life* based on the writings of Alice Bailey.

5. The Almighty God.

6. It is important to distinguish between the **Christos** and the Christ. The Christos is the Christ Energy. While the Creator is at the centre of the Universe, the Christos surrounds the Creator. The Christ was the physical embodiment of the Christos.

7. Particles of awareness which are divinely illuminated and which are aspects of God.

Chapter VII

1. **The over-soul** is the supreme, universal Soul — Almighty God.

2. **Nihilism** is a view where nothing is believed in, except materialism and science.

Chapter VIII

1. **The Solar Logos** are particles of awareness which are already illuminated and have a specific understanding of what they are. They interact with different vehicles which manifest in their space, e.g. the planets of the Solar System, and different energy beings within their orbit.

2. **The Living Library** refers to all of the frequencies donated into the Planet and which can be accessed by the 'librarians' currently incarnate on Earth. See also *Note 9* (Chapter III).

3. **Silent DNA** refers to physical DNA which is not transcribed or expressed in the cell. Over 90% of the human genome appears to be silent and does not apparently encode any proteins. It remains a major scientific mystery as to the function or use of these vast tracts of DNA.

4. *Symphonies of the Planets* are recordings taken from the NASA Voyager spacecraft as it travelled through the Solar System.

5. Broadly speaking, **channelling** means to bring through into the physical different frequencies or information. In one sense, it can be said that we channel all the time because we act as channels for the divine within us. In this context, chanelling means to connect and bring through a series of frequencies which are then interpreted through our sensory and neural system. Because the channel is conscious and aware of what he or she is bringing through, there is inevitably a degree of interpretation in this process. See also *Note 24* (Chapter III).

Chapter IX

1. **The Akashic record** is the sum total of the experiences of the soul aspect held within its memory banks. This memory bank is stored on a single permanent atom which is left behind in the physical when a person dies. Accessing this memory bank provides information on all the past lives of an individual.

Glossary

The Avatar

> The Avatar is the total manifestation of God in human form on Earth, as the Eternal Living Perfect Master. The Avatar was the first individual soul to emerge from the evolutionary and involutionary process as the Perfect Master, and He is the only One who has ever manifested, or will ever manifest. The Avatar incarnates either every 700 years or every 1400 years, being called into physicality by the five Perfect Masters present on Earth at that time. Whenever the Avatar manifests on Earth, His Godhood gives a universal push, and the result is universal. Depending upon the time period, the Avatar appears in different forms, under different names, in different parts of the world. His appearance always coincides with the spiritual regeneration of humankind. We are currently in an Avataric period which lasts for 100 years after the Avatar drops His Physical Form.

> Each Avatar will have a specific personality. Meher Baba's focus was inward. He generally worked with small groups. However, everything the Avatar does is symbolic, and every action performed in the physical will have a manifestation astrally and mentally.

Chakras

> There are seven main chakra centres in the body. These are the base (or root), sexual (or hara), solar plexus, heart, throat, third eye, and crown. Each chakra has a particular vibration, and gives off a sound, a pitch, a taste, and a smell. Each chakra also has a colour, which will vary from time to time. Chakras are energy centres, and function as dimensional doorways between the different energy systems of the body, so that the outer physical manifestation of a chakra has a representation within the chakra systems of the subtle bodies. The chakras should be balanced, and should work in harmony with each other, but there are frequent imbalances to be found within a person's chakra system. Each chakra is associated

with a particular quality or activity. Thus the root chakra is associated with survival; the sexual chakra with sexual energy; the solar plexus chakra with emotions; the heart chakra with being centred, and with love vibrations; the throat chakra with communication; the third eye with seeing within; and the crown chakra with spirituality. (This description of the chakras is something of a simplification, and different cultures have different interpretations.)

The body also has a series of minor chakra centres which are energy portals, such as in the palms of the hands, the soles of the feet, and the knees.

Crystal Skulls

The Crystal Skulls are artefacts which were seeded into the Planet almost 90,000 years ago. They are amplification devices, and keys to specific crystalline frequencies. They form a direct connection with the Divine. These crystalline frequencies focus on harmony, truth, light, love, understanding, and compassion, although each Skull has a specific keying-in frequency of its own. The most notable example is the Mitchell-Hedges Crystal Skull, which was found by Anna Mitchell-Hedges and is currently located in Canada.

Devas

Every life form has its Deva — an alternative life form, which holds cell structure together. The Devas' awareness is very different from our own, and they develop and grow through feeling, rather than through the power of conscious thought. They are the qualities and attributes of matter.

Dimensional Doorways

Dimensional doorways are effectively gates or portals from one dimension to another. They can be doorways through time or space, and can connect with different levels on the inner planes. In a very real sense, the heart chakra and the third eye are dimensional doorways into the different plane levels. Dimensional doorways can be of many different shapes and sizes, and can be accessed in a variety of different ways. Just as there are positive doors of intent, so there are also negative doorways, which give access to slower frequencies. New doorways are needed at the present time, in order to give access to the Planet through the 'ring-pass-not', which is a band of blue light encircling the Earth. Incarnating soul aspects entering the Planet pass through the 'ring-pass-not', which acts as an eraser of past memories: each soul aspect therefore enters with a severe case of spiritual amnesia. The 'ring-pass-not' acts as a barrier to the free movement of energy and information to the Planet, and the construction of dimensional doorways through this barrier is therefore particularly necessary.

Divine Fire

This refers to a type of energy that will enter the Planet through the Mind of One. Fire energy is also manifest at many different levels, and through different aspects of Devic, Elemental, Solar, and Planetary awareness. A more detailed analysis of the different types of Fire can be found in *A Treatise on Cosmic Fire* by Alice Bailey.

Frequencies

Frequencies are the vibratory notes or signals which are held by all bodies, both animate and inanimate. These frequencies can vibrate across a whole vibratory spectrum, from high to low. A slow frequency, or negative frequency note, can be represented by emotions such as fear, anger, or depression; such energies often stem from old disharmonies. For example, sites of old battles will hold slow frequency notes from the past. Higher frequency vibrations are represented by emotions such as joy, and feelings of harmony. Frequency notes can also be viewed within the context of light and dark, indicating the alignment of frequencies being worked with.

Guides

A guide is a source of energy external to the human personality. It is also an intelligence which communicates with individuals in the physical realms, and generally assists them in following a path which is in their best interest. Guides come in many shapes and forms, and can work etherically, astrally, mentally, or sometimes on a soul level. Since there are millions of sub-planes, there are many different types of guides, ranging from those who may appear more 'familiar', such as Native American Indian, Chinese, Ancient Roman, or Zulu, through to the more extra-terrestrial forms, and to the highest form of guide, which is a Perfect Master or Avatar. Specific guides may often be associated with an individual over many of that person's lifetimes, and they will gain from the experience of working with those in physical matter. Guides also have to be trained, and so different guides will have different levels of expertise and experience. Learning to connect with and recognise one's guides is an important discipline, and one that will be very beneficial.

Karma and Karmic Charge

The word 'Karma' means 'action', 'work', 'effect', and 'fate'. In simple terms, the natural and necessary happenings in one's life are preconditioned by one's past actions, in this life and in previous lives.

Karma affects every life form in physical matter. It can be both positive and negative, and can operate on the physical, astral, and mental planes. An individual may have worked off a large amount of physical karma over many lifetimes, but may still have astral or mental karma to work through. The overwhelming majority of people whom you meet will be connected to you through karma. If you have encountered a particular individual over many lifetimes, it is possible to generate a substantial amount of mutual karma, often both positive and negative, which can form 'karmic knots' which are difficult to unravel. In clearing this karmic association, it is often necessary to work back to the life where the over-riding karmic charge was originally established, and then to clear this out, thus allowing the karmic knot to dissipate energetically. This is one of the reasons why David Cousins describes karma as "an active form of denial, reinforced by judgement". In short, karma directly influences all of our experiences.

Once an individual perceives the personal choices, and commits to the process of transmutation of individual karma, it will eventually be possible to bring about a balance of positive and negative karma, thereby freeing that person from the laws of rebirth. It is also worth remembering that karma can operate on many different levels — personal, group, planetary, solar system, and galactic.

Mind of One

The Mind of One is a thought form that has been created by God, and which is being realised through the Spiritual Hierarchy and light workers. It represents the group alignment, and the necessity for merging and unification of purpose and action by all light workers. Connecting with the Mind of One is rather like tapping into the light workers' super-computer, since it provides information, power, love, unity, and a vast array of frequencies.

Perfect Masters

A Perfect Master is a God-Realised soul who retains God-Consciousness and creation-consciousness simultaneously, and who works within creation to help souls towards the realisation of God. A Perfect Master is the highest and most exalted divine status of God in human form. There are five of them in physical matter at any one time. The Perfect Master consciously experiences not only infinite knowledge, but also infinite power, infinite bliss, and all-goodness. A Perfect Master is one who not only becomes God, but who, after achieving God-Realisation, also comes down to the ordinary normal consciousness of humanity. He possesses simultaneously God-Consciousness and mental, subtle, and gross consciousness.

Photon Belt and Photon Energy

The Photon Belt is a band of high-energy light or photon energy. It is approximately 256 million light years across. Earth travels through this belt every 26 thousand years, and we recently entered it (in 1998), although the preliminary effects of the Photon Belt could be felt earlier than this. No one is precisely sure when we will be in the epicentre of its effects, nor what these effects will be, although it is apparent that the photon field of energy will impact upon both our physical bodies and our emotional experiences. One direct result of this incoming wave of light is the opening of the astral levels.

Planes of Consciousness

The planes of consciousness, which are also known as the planes of involution of consciousness, are the states of consciousness experienced by the soul while traversing the spiritual path (reference is also made to the 'inner planes', which is a short-hand description of the planes of consciousness). There are seven planes in all, with millions of sub-planes, the first six planes being the focus of the soul's journey before becoming God-Realised. During the first six planes, the soul gradually withdraws the focus of its consciousness from the gross sphere (the physical) to the subtle sphere, and thence to the mental sphere. This is involution. The subtle sphere consists of the first four planes of consciousness as experienced by the subtle (or astral) body through one's subtle impressions, which are less dense than the gross impressions. The fourth plane serves as the threshold to the mental sphere (the fifth and sixth planes), but is neither fully subtle nor fully mental. The mental sphere is experienced by the mental body through one's mental impressions, which are much finer than the subtle impressions. At the seventh plane, the soul experiences Realisation, and knows itself to be God.

Reincarnation

A soul aspect entering the physical plane must work its way through all the permutations of matter, through minerals, and then through plants and animals, before it eventually can incarnate in the human form. Once it has reached the human stage of progress, each soul aspect has on average 8,400,000 lifetimes during which to explore the physical realms, and to complete its cycle up through the planes. This process of birth and re-birth is known as reincarnation.

Root Races

The Root Races represent major permutations or cycles of energy within form which have been present on Earth. A Root Race will have a particular focus in terms of energy, body form, chakra alignment, and arrangement of physical, etheric, astral, and mental bodies. The beginning and end of each Root Race has coincided usually with major changes on the Planet and the destruction of the form of the old Root Race. What is unique about the transition from the fifth to the sixth Root Race, is that the human body form is being retained and modified.

Soul

A soul is created by separation from the Divine Ocean. It then begins a process of becoming aware of itself as being separate from the Source. Most souls, as they begin their downward journey into different realities, split themselves into seven aspects, with each aspect then splitting into two, thus providing the soul with the capacity to acquire as much information as possible. Soul aspects have the same vibratory structure within the genetic background of the soul. The soul's full cycle is for all of its aspects to separate from the Source, which is timeless; moving into outer time; working downwards through the various levels into the gross physical matter; and then rising in an upward spiral, and returning to the Source, where the soul aspects merge back into one. It usually takes millions of years and 8,400,000 lives for the soul to complete this journey. A number of soul aspects can be incarnated on the Planet at any one time, up to a maximum of five. It is possible for one soul aspect to encounter another soul aspect as human beings. This is the true meaning of what it is to meet a 'soul-mate' and the energy interchange between these two soul aspects will be considerable and often life-changing.

Subtle Bodies

Subtle bodies are representations of the vital energy force. They function in the inner planes, and provide the soul with a series of experiences. These experiences are like reference points for the soul aspects, as they work within a multi-dimensional context and represent aspects of desire. Subtle bodies are also a series of records of what each soul aspect has encountered, and they form part of the process of transmutation and release, through the soul's act of becoming desireless as a result of experience. Subtle bodies are built up by the soul aspect on its downward journey, and provide a series of filters for that soul aspect in each dimension in which it has an interest. Similarly, the soul aspect will build up further bodies as part of its upward journey, although as this journey progresses, there is a need to bring all of these different subtle bodies together as part of the re-bonding process. A large number of subtle bodies can be found within the different planes. As one progresses up the planes, the subtle bodies become larger and larger as more space is encountered. When referring to subtle bodies, it is also common to refer to the astral and mental bodies.

Thought Forms

A thought form is a vibrational package which is initiated by mental output, and which attracts astral or emotional energy. Thought forms are maintained by energy input, both consciously and subliminally. They are fed by the way in which we think and behave, and especially by our internal thoughts. Thought forms can be negatively or positively charged, depending on the impulse of the individual at the time. Since very few people are able to shut off their 'internal dialogue' for any length of time, then it follows that humanity is generating a massive outpouring of thought-structures at any given point in time. These thought-structures will span an octave of energy, from the very negative to the very positive, and the individual has a choice of whether or not to link into a particular point on this octave. If you link in near the bottom, then you will be linking into aggression, fear, tyranny, and suicide. As you connect with the more positive end of the spectrum, then happiness, joy, understanding, peace, and harmony will be much more evident.

Given that energy follows thought, there is a way in which everything we see and perceive is a thought form, ranging from our daily moods, to a physical object, to the banking system, the Euro, and even the Earth. Thought forms can be held within our personal auric fields for long periods of time. If many negative thought forms are held in this way, then an individual can be locked into a particular stream of thought.

Bibliography

Adilakshmi
The Mother.
(1994) Mother Meera Publications.

Bailey, Alice A.
A Treatise on Cosmic Fire.
(1995) Lucis Publishing Company.

The Seven Rays of Life.
(1995) Lucis Publishing Company.

Ponder on This.
(1996) Lucis Publishing Company.

A Treatise on White Magic.
(1997) Lucis Publishing Company.

Brennan, Barbara A.
Light Emerging. The Journey of Personal Healing.
(1993) Bantam Books.

Cousins, David A.
Handbook for Light Workers.
(1993) Barton House.

Duce, Ivy O.
How A Master Works.
(1975) Sufism Reoriented.

Jessawala, Eruch
That's How It Was. Stories of Life With Meher Baba.
(1995) Sheriar Foundation.

Hattiangadi, Shaila
Sai's Story.
(1998) Sai Towers Publishing.

Marciniak, Barbara

Bringers of the Dawn. Teachings from the Pleiadians.
(1992) Bear & Company.

Earth: Pleiadian Keys to the Living Library.
(1995) Bear & Company.

Meher Baba

God Speaks. The Theme of Creation and its Purpose.
(1973) Dodd, Mead & Company.

Discourses.
(1995) Sheriar Foundation.

Mother Meera

Answers.
(1991) Rider.

Answers Part II.
(1997) Mother Meera Publications.

Natu, Bal

The Samadhi. Star of Infinity.
(1997) Sheriar Foundation.

Padmanaban, R.

Love is My Form. A Biographical Series on Sri Sathya Sai Baba.
Volume I. The Advent (1926-1950).
(2000) Sai Towers Publishing.

Ramakrishnan, K.K. (Ed.)

Sai Baba. The Perfect Master.
(1991) Meher Era Publications, Pune.

Stevens, D.E.

Listen Humanity. Meher Baba.
(1989) Companion Books.

ʒananda, Paramahansa

Autobiography of a Yogi.
(1993) Self-Realization Fellowship.

N ick Scott-Ram studied Natural Sciences at Cambridge University and subsequently completed his PhD in the Philosophy of Science there. He has worked in the biotechnology industry for over 15 years and has also qualified as a cranio-sacral therapist. Over the years he has developed a deep interest in working with different types of meditation and exploring the subtle energies 'within us'.

Additional information on Books, Workshops and
Other Activities can be found on the following
web-sites:
www.devictruth.com
www.soulspeaks.co.uk